THE
HOUSEPLA
LIBRARY

GU00982970

FRAGR
PLANTS

Kenneth A. Beckett

Salem House

All rights reserved: no part of this publication
may be reproduced, stored in a retrieval system, or transmitted
in any form or by any means, electronic, mechanical,
photocopying or otherwise, without the prior
written permission of the Publishers.

First published in the United States by
Salem House Publishers, 1989, 462 Boston Street,
Topsfield, Massachusetts, 01983.

Text and photographs copyright © Kenneth A. Beckett 1989

Copyright © Swallow Publishing Ltd 1989

Conceived and produced by
Swallow Books, 260 Pentonville Road,
London N1 9JY

ISBN: 0 88162 382 2
Art Director: Elaine Partington
Editor: Catherine Tilley
Designers: Jean Hoyes and Hilary Krag
Studio: Del & Co
Typesetters: Bournetype, Bournemouth
Printed in Italy by Imago Publishing Limited

Author's acknowledgments
The great majority of pictures in this book are of plants
growing in botanical and private gardens. My wife Gillian,
who took most of the colour transparencies, and I are
particularly grateful to the following people for their
cooperation in allowing us access to their plant
collections behind the scenes: Mr C. D. Brickell, formerly
Director of the RHS Gardens, Wisley, Dr R. D. Shaw,
Curator of the Royal Botanic Garden, Edinburgh and
Mr J. B. E. Simmons, Curator of the Royal Botanic
Gardens, Kew. We are especially indebted to
Mr L. Maurice Mason for allowing us unlimited time
among his treasures at Talbot Manor, Fincham, Norfolk
over the years. As a result, more of his plants feature in
this book than anyone else's.

INTRODUCTION

For many people, the most important consideration when choosing a plant for the home or garden is its overall appearance and especially the colour and shape of its flowers. The plant's fragrance is very much an afterthought, but what a delightful bonus it can be – a room filled with the scent of jasmine or *Hoya* will certainly make a greater impact than the sight of a few pretty flowers.

Unfortunately, comparatively few of the well-known, easily grown houseplants have scent; nevertheless, all the species described here can be kept successfully in the home, at least in the short term. After flowering it is usually best to return them to a conservatory or greenhouse, or even outside during the summer, to recuperate. However, with proper care many of the plants will happily live indoors permanently and, indeed, deserve to be seen in this environment more than they usually are.

Just as beauty is in the eye of the beholder, so the appreciation of scent depends upon each individual's nose. A strong, sweet or pleasant smell to one person may be almost unnoticeable or overpowering and unpleasant to another. There are further complications in introducing fragrance to the home: most of the lighter scents need humid air to carry well. In the conservatory or greenhouse the perfume may be strong, but when the plant is brought into a dry indoor atmosphere, it can seem to fade or disappear, at least to some people.

Siting, choosing and buying

When selecting a plant for the home, make sure it is suitable for the position you have in mind. There is no point in selecting a sun lover for a shady corner, or a tropical plant for a cool room. Basic information on the light, heat and water requirements of all the plants described in this book are given in easily understood symbols at the beginning of each entry.

The quality of houseplants, whether purchased from a nursery, garden centre or multiple store, is now, generally, very good. It makes sense, however, to choose only the best plants and to shop around if need be. Do not buy plants which look pale and weak, or have limp, flecked or crippled leaves. If the plant has flowers or buds, make sure they do not fall easily when it is gently shaken. In winter, get a new plant home as soon as possible, as prolonged chilling can cause partial or total shrivelling or falling of leaves and flower buds.

Watering

Giving pot plants too much or too little water is the most common cause of root failure and subsequent death. For the beginner, knowing when to water a houseplant can be a major problem. Aim to keep the soil moist, but not wet. Too much water will result in a sour, constantly wet soil that will cause root rot and the collapse of the plant. Too little water produces a slow-growing plant which is very prone to wilt and prematurely shed its leaves and flower buds. The easiest way to decide when a pot plant needs water is to probe the soil surface to a depth of about 1cm (½in) with the tip of your finger. If the soil feels barely moist give the plant a thorough watering, filling up the gap between the soil surface and the pot rim.

Humidity

Most houseplants come from countries where the air is humid for much of the year as a result of frequent rainfall. Although many species are remarkably tolerant of the dry air in modern homes, even they will be healthier and better looking in more moist air. The humidity can be increased by standing the plants on trays of gravel filled with water to just below the gravel surface. The water level must be topped up regularly but never be allowed to overlap the pot base. Alternatively, plunge the pots up to their rims in deep containers of moist peat. Another method is to use a fine droplet (mist) sprayer to wet the leaves at least once a day, except when temperatures drop below the average minimum.

Feeding

A plant's potting soil will eventually become exhausted of nutrients, and the plant will begin to starve, despite being fed regularly. Growth will slow to a standstill, the lower leaves will often fall and all the young leaves will look noticeably small and pale, or take on tints of red or purple. Flowering will also slow down and often cease, or the buds may even fall without opening. Before a plant reaches this extreme state of starvation, corrective feeding should begin. This is best achieved by applying one of the several liquid feeds, readily available in garden centres and used according to makers' instructions. For a quick tonic, the so-called foliar feeds are well worth considering. These contain highly soluble fertilizers, plus a wetting agent, which are mixed with water and sprayed on the leaves.

Top-dressing

Plants that are kept in pots for a long time should be top-dressed every spring. Use a small hand fork or a large kitchen fork to strip away the top layer of soil and small roots and so remove about one-sixth to one-quarter of the total depth of the root ball. Do not damage the larger roots. Replace the discarded layer with fresh soil, ideally containing one of the slow-release fertilizers. Finally, gently firm the soil around the plant and water well.

Pruning

Climbers and shrubs have a tendency to grow too large, and will need cutting back from time to time. They are best thinned out to let in light and air, and to eliminate thin, weakly growth, when dormant or after flowering. This is most easily done by cutting out the oldest whole branches or stems down to their bases. The remaining growth can then be shortened by one-quarter to one-third of the length. Evergreen perennials, such as *Asparagus*, can be dealt with in much the same way. Deciduous or semi-deciduous perennials, for example *Hymenocallis*, should be cut back to ground level when the foliage becomes yellow.

Orchids

The orchids, which feature prominently in this book because of their scented flowers, are epiphytes, that is, they grow perched on another plant, and need somewhat different treatment. In the wild they cling to tree branches and mossy rocks, gaining their sustenance from decayed moss, wind-blown humus and rain. When cultivated, they need well-aerated containers and rooting media. Containers should ideally be custom-made slatted wooden baskets or perforated pots. Ordinary clay pots can be used, but must be two-thirds filled with drainage material, ideally, pieces of broken clay pots. If possible, hang up the containers so that air can circulate all around the plants. An easily made rooting medium is one or two parts bark or polystyrene chips, two parts sphagnum moss and one part rough peat. This mixture should be poured around the roots, and the container tapped gently on a hard surface to settle it (firming is not needed). Only water when the rooting medium dries out. Liquid feed should be applied at half-standard strength to plants that have been established for at least one year. Humidity is essential, and the plants must be mist-sprayed at least once a day (unless temperatures are abnormally low), and twice ideally.

'Western Rose', a *Cymbidium* hybrid (see page 22)

How to use this book

This book contains a selection of the most suitable and readily available fragrant plants, together with descriptions of the plants in their mature state, and their requirements (temperature, watering, and so on). These are given in the symbols which are explained below. From this, you should be able to select a plant which meets your requirements exactly, and which will thrive in your home or conservatory. Although, as far as possible, technical terms have not been used in the main text of the book, there have been occasions when it has been impossible to avoid them. They are all explained in full in the glossary on page 63.

Symbol key

Cultural requirements and overall plant shape/growth habit are summarized in the form of at-a-glance symbols beside each entry. These provide quick reference and supplement the main description of the plant.

Temperature requirements

 Tropical/warm – minimum 15–18°C (60–65°F)

 Temperate – minimum 10–15°C (50–60°F)

 Cool – minimum 5–10°C (40–50°F); down to −3°C (27°F) if noted as hardy

Light requirements

 Full sun

 Partial shade

 Full shade

Watering requirements

 Light – Allow rooting medium to dry out completely between waterings.

 Medium – Allow surface of rooting medium to dry out between waterings.

 Heavy – Keep entire rooting medium moist at all times.

Plant habit/shape

 Erect

 Spreading/prostrate

 Mat-forming

 Bushy

 Weeping

 Climbing/Scrambling

 Rosette-forming

 Pendent/Trailing

 Tufted/Fan-like/ Clump-forming

 Globular (or cylindrical)

ACOKANTHERA
Apocynaceae

Origin: *Southern to tropical East Africa and Arabia. A genus of evergreen trees and shrubs characterized by opposite pairs of lance-shaped to oval leaves with clusters of five-lobed, tubular, fragrant flowers borne in their axils. Flowers set to form oval to globe-shaped, poisonous berries. The species described is best grown in a large container and, once bloomed, may have its flowered stems cut back by half. It is best in the conservatory, being more effective in bloom when of a good size. Propagate by seed in spring or by cuttings in summer.* Acokanthera *derives from the Greek words* akis *and* anthera *meaning spike and anther, referring to the pointed nature of the anthers.*

Acokanthera spectabilis

Species cultivated
A. spectabilis Wintersweet South Africa
A tree growing to 5m (16ft) in the wild, but smaller and shrubby in cultivation. Oblong to lance-shaped, firm textured, glossy deep green leaves which provide a foil for the 2cm (¾in) wide, white flowers opening from winter to spring. They are followed by poisonous, purple-black berries, produced freely even when plants are small.

ANGRAECUM
Orchidaceae

Origin: *Tropical and sub-tropical areas of Africa, Malagasy, Indian Ocean islands and the Philippines. A genus of 220 species of orchids that grow perched on trees (epiphytic) which do not produce pseudobulbs. They generally have erect stems bearing two rows of*

Angraecum sesquipedale

fleshy, strap-shaped to narrowly oval leaves. Flowers can be quite large, are usually carried in racemes but are occasionally solitary, and are mostly white and green, or sometimes yellow; they are starry and have a lip with a slender spur which is often elongated to great length. Plants can be grown in the home, but are best in a conservatory since they need more humidity than can normally be provided indoors. Propagate by cuttings of well-grown side shoots in late spring. Angraecum *derives from the Malaysian name* angurek.

Species cultivated

A. sesquipedale Malagasy

Stems are erect and robust, growing to 60cm (2ft) or more. Leaves are dark, almost blue-green, reaching 30cm (1ft) in length. The leaf tips are bi-lobed, the two lobes of unequal size. Flowers are fragrant, fleshy textured, ivory white, growing to 18cm (7in) across with a heart-shaped lip and 25cm (10in) spur. Flowers are borne in winter.

ARDISIA

Myrsinaceae

Ardisia crispa

Origin: *Tropics and sub-tropics; mostly from Asia and America, some in Australia. A genus of 400 evergreen shrubs and trees. They usually have alternate elliptic to lance-shaped leaves and small flowers in clusters or at the ends of the stems. Propagate by seed or heel cuttings in spring and summer.* Ardisia *derives from the Greek* ardis, *a point – the anthers are spear-pointed.*

Species cultivated

A. crispa (*A. crenata, A. crenulata*) Marlberry, Coralberry, Spiceberry S.E. Asia

A shrub growing to 1.5m (5ft). Leaves are oblong and lance-shaped, 5–10cm (2–4in) in length with wavy edges. Flowers are five-petalled, starry, fragrant, white sometimes flushed with red, and clustered at the ends of the branches. Fruits are bright red, rounded and 6–8mm (¼–⅓in) in diameter.

ARISAEMA

Araceae

Origin: *Mostly E. Africa and Asia; a few in North America. A genus of 150 species of perennials with tuberous or rhizomatous roots. Each plant generally has just one or two long-stalked leaves, the leaf blade being pedately divided into three to 15 leaflets or lobes. The flowers are tiny and petalless, the males having two to five stamens; they are borne on a spadix and surrounded by a spathe. Though best grown*

Arisaema candidissimum

in a conservatory, these plants can be flowered in the home. *Propagate by offsets at potting time or by seed (sown when ripe if possible).*

Arisaema *derives from the Greek* aris, arum *and* haima, *blood, used in the sense of a blood relationship with arum.*

Species cultivated

A. candidissimum China

Leaves grow solitarily on a stalk to 30cm (1ft). They are trifoliate, with 8–20cm (3–8in) long, broadly oval leaflets. Spathes are hooded, 7–10cm (2¾–4in) long, white striped with green on the back and beautifully tinged with pink inside; they appear in early summer before the leaf unfurls.

ASPARAGUS
Liliaceae

Asparagus falcatus

Origin: *Europe, Africa, Asia and Australia. A genus of 30 species of climbing, sprawling and upright plants, some herbaceous, some shrubby. They are distinguished by the absence of true leaves, their place being taken by needle-like, awl-shaped or broader leaf-like stems; the true leaves are reduced to tiny scales. The flowers are small, either starry or bell-shaped, with six tepals and are followed by berries. Propagate by division or by seed in spring. The species below make good long-term house or conservatory plants.* Asparagus *derives from the ancient Greek name for the genus.*

Species cultivated

A. densiflorus South Africa

Tuberous-rooted, tufted; stems growing to 1.2m (4ft) or more long, arching or hanging, with many branches. The leaf-like stems are usually solitary, very narrow, 1–2cm (⅜–¾in) long, bright green. Flowers are white, pink tinted, in short racemes; fruits are bright red. *A.d.* 'Sprengeri' (*A. sprengeri*) is similar to the type, but its leaf-like stems grow in clusters of one to six (usually three).

A. falcatus Sicklethorn South Africa, Sri Lanka

A twining evergreen climber reaching 4m (13ft) or so. The leaf-like stems are 4–5cm (1½–2in) long, lance- to sickle-shaped, bright green, and borne in clusters of three or more along the pale stems. Flowers are white, tiny, growing in axillary racemes 5cm (2in) long.

BEAUMONTIA
Apocynaceae

Origin: *Indo-Malaysia, China. A genus of possibly 15 species of woody-stemmed climbers, only one of which is in general cultivation. Although normally a high-climbing, vigorous species it responds well to being kept in a container and will bloom when fairly small. To stimulate the plant to flower, it must receive winter night temperatures in the 7–10°C (45–50°F) range, or even a little below this, and, at the same time, must be kept on the dry side. To restrict size, prune immediately after flowering. Propagate by cuttings in late summer.* Beaumontia *commemorates Lady Diana Beaumont (d. 1831) of Bretton Hall, Yorkshire.*

Species cultivated

B. grandiflora N. India

In containers this plant can be kept to a height of 2–3m (6½–10ft), but it is capable, when planted out, of attaining twice this and more. The

handsome leaves are 13–20cm (5–8in) long, oval-oblong, deep lustrous green above, red-brown hairy beneath. Flowers are 10–13cm (4–5in) wide, trumpet-shaped with five spreading petal lobes, white, fragrant, opening in small clusters in summer.

Beaumontia grandiflora

BORONIA
Rutaceae

Origin: *Australia. A genus of 70 species of evergreen shrubs. They are generally small to medium-sized, slender-stemmed plants with opposite, undivided or pinnate leaves and small four-petalled, somewhat flesby-textured flowers in axillary clusters. They are attractive pot plants for a sunny window or conservatory, flowering in spring. With pruning they can be kept compact. Propagate by seed in spring or by cuttings with a heel in late summer.* Boronia *was named for Francesco Borone (1769–1794), an Italian plant collector who worked for Dr Adam Afzelius in Sierra Leone, Professor John Sibthorp in Greece and Sir J.E. Smith in various parts of Europe.*

Boronia citriodora

Species cultivated

B. citriodora Tasmania
A spreading shrub, rarely growing above 30cm (1ft) tall. Leaves are lemon-scented, with undivided pinna, composed of three to seven lance-shaped, thick-textured leaflets each up to 1.5cm (⅝in) long. Flowers are star-shaped, soft pink, 1–1.5cm (⅜–⅝in) wide, opening in clusters from the upper leaf axils in spring. This mountain species is the hardiest in cultivation, and will stand light frost in winter.

B. megastigma Western Australia
A low shrub growing to a height of about 30–60cm (1–2ft). Leaves have three to five very narrow leaflets 8–18mm (⅓–¾in) long. Flowers are 1–1.2cm (⅜–½in) wide, strongly fragrant, rich purple-brown outside and yellow within. They are borne singly from the upper leaf axils.

BRUNFELSIA
Solanaceae

Brunfelsia americana

Origin: *Tropical America and West Indies. A genus of 30 species of evergreen shrubs with alternate, elliptic, oval to lance-shaped, leathery leaves and long-tubed flowers, spreading at the mouth to five broad lobes. They are useful flowering shrubs, needing shade from the hottest sun and a humid atmosphere. Keep leading shoots pinched out for a shapely specimen. Propagate by cuttings, preferably with a heel, in a case with bottom heat.* Brunfelsia *was named for Otto Brunfels (1489–1534), a German physician, botanist and Carthusian monk, who produced some of the earliest good drawings of plants.*

Species cultivated
B. americana (*B. violacea*) Lady of the night South America
A shrubby plant, reaching 3m (10ft) or more in height. Leaves are oval to elliptic, 4–13cm (1½–5in) long. Flowers are trumpet-shaped, growing to a length of 8cm (3in), opening yellow and fading to white. They are carried singly and are fragrant at night.

BUDDLEIA (BUDDLEJA)
Buddlejaceae (Loganiaceae)

Origin: *Temperate and sub-tropical areas of Asia, America and South Africa; most frequent in Asia. A genus of 100 species of deciduous or evergreen shrubs or small trees. They have opposite pairs of leaves, occasionally alternate, which are oblong-oval to lance-shaped, and small, four-petalled, tubular flowers in pyramid-shaped panicles. Most species are hardy, but the one described makes a good pot or tub plant for a light room or conservatory. Propagate by cuttings, preferably with a heel, taken in late summer.* Buddleia *was named for the Rev. Adam Buddle (1660–1715), Vicar of Fambridge in Essex and a noted botanist.*

Species cultivated
B. asiatica East Indies, China
A slender, evergreen shrub growing to 3m (10ft) or more. Leaves are lance-shaped, 10–20cm (4–8in) long, sometimes toothed and white-

downy beneath. Flowers are about 6mm (¼in) wide carried in dense, drooping, cylindrical panicles reaching a length of 15cm (6in), from late winter to spring.

Buddleia asiatica

CARICA
Caricaceae

Origin: *Tropical to warm temperate Americas. A genus of about 40 species of trees, shrubs and climbers. The one species described below is widely grown in tropical countries for its fruit, but if grown simply as an ornamental fruit it makes an unusual foliage plant. Seeds are sometimes available from seedsmen or can be extracted from shop-bought fruits. Sow in spring at not less than 24–30°C (75–87°F). Carica derives from the Greek karike, a fig-like plant; used by Linnaeus on account of its fig-like leaves.*

Species cultivated
C. papaya Pawpaw, Papaya Not known truly wild but probably originating in southern Mexico and Costa Rica

A small tree growing to 3m (10ft) in containers, 5–10m (16–33ft) tall in the open tropical garden. The stem is usually pole-like and without branches, sometimes with a few lateral stems. The long-stalked leaves grow at the top in a palm-like cluster; leaf blades are shaped like an outspread hand, more or less disc-like in outline, growing to 60cm (2ft) wide, and divided into seven to 11 deeply cleft or toothed lobes. Flowers are trumpet-shaped, about 2.5cm (1in) long, cream or yellow in the leaf axils, fragrant, borne in summer. Plants are of single sex, the males with hanging flower trusses 25–75cm (10–30in) long, the females in small, short-stemmed clusters, or solitary.

Carica papaya

CARISSA
Apocynaceae

Carissa grandiflora

Origin: *Warm temperate and sub-tropical regions of Africa, Asia and Australia. A genus of 35 species of evergreen shrubs. They have opposite, leathery leaves and bear thorns, which can be branched. The tubular, five-petalled flowers can be fragrant and are followed by berries, which in many species are edible. They make good tub plants. Propagate by seed in spring or by heel cuttings in summer (ideally with bottom heat). Carissa is a Latin form of the Indian common name.*

Species cultivated

C. grandiflora Natal plum South Africa
An evergreen shrub growing to 5m (16ft) in the wild, but rarely exceeding 2m (6½ft) in a tub. Leaves are broadly oval, 2.5–8cm (1–3in) long. Flowers are 8–12mm (⅓–½in) long, white, carried singly or in small cymes in late spring and very fragrant. *C.g.* 'Nana' ('Minima') has a dwarf, compact habit and is best for growing in a pot.

CATTLEYA
Orchidaceae

Cattleya loddigesii

Origin: *Warmer regions of the Americas from South America to Mexico, including the West Indies. A genus of 60 species of orchids that grow perched on trees (epiphytic). The narrowly leathery leaves arise from cylindrical to flattened pseudobulbs and the flowers are often large and showy. All make excellent conservatory plants and thrive well in a sunny window, provided the atmosphere is not too dry. Give some shade from the hottest sun in summer. Propagate by division at potting time. Cattleya was named for William Cattley (d. 1832), a collector and grower of rare plants.*

Species cultivated

C. citrina Tulip cattleya Mexico
Rounded to egg-shaped, silvery-green pseudobulbs, about 5cm (2in) tall, bearing two or three strap-shaped hanging leaves each to 20cm (8in) long. Flowers are 7–9cm (2¾–3½in) long, opening to a tulip-like bell, fragrant, citron-yellow in colour with a golden lip; they are borne singly or in pairs on a hanging stalk from autumn to spring.
C. harrisoniana See *C. loddigesii.*
C. loddigesii Brazil, Paraguay
Pseudobulbs, which are cylindrical, grow to 45cm (1½ft). There are two leaves, which are narrowly elliptic, leathery, reaching 15cm (6in). Flowers grow to 11cm (4½in) wide, wavy-textured, bluish pink to

lilac-rose, the lip darker pink, cream or pale yellow at the base, borne in two- to six-flowered racemes from late summer to autumn.

CESTRUM
Solanaceae

Origin: *Mexico to Chile, West Indies. A genus of 150 species of shrubs, most of which are evergreen. They have alternate, lance-shaped to oval leaves and tubular, somewhat inflated flowers borne in nodding or arching panicles at the ends of the stems. Each flower has five pointed, petal lobes at the mouth. They are followed by red to purple-black berries. Cestrums make good tub plants for the conservatory, where they are best trained to wires on the back wall and under the roof. Two- and three-year-old stems produce the best flowers, so cut third-year stems back to the base at the end of their season. Propagate by heel cuttings in late summer in warmth, or by seed in spring.* Cestrum *derives from an ancient Greek name for an unknown species, used by Linnaeus.*

Species cultivated

C. aurantiacum Guatemala
An evergreen semi-climbing shrub growing to 3m (10ft). Leaves are oval and 5–9cm (2–3½in) long. The bright-orange flowers are 2cm (¾in) long with abruptly bent back lobes, stalkless, borne in leafy panicles at the ends of the stems in summer; their fragrance is most apparent at night.

Cestrum aurantiacum

× *Citrofortunella mitis*

× CITROFORTUNELLA

Rutaceae

Origin: *A hybrid arisen in cultivation. A hybrid genus combining species of* Citrus *and* Fortunella. *Three species are known, one of which is frequently met with. They are intermediate between their parents and the one described below makes an attractive pot plant. Propagate by cuttings with a heel in late summer.*

Species cultivated

× **C. mitis** (*Citrus mitis*) (*Citrus reticulata* [tangerine] × *Fortunella* [kumquat]) Calamondin

An evergreen shrub growing to 2m (6½ft), usually less in a pot. Leaves are 4–6cm (1½–2½in) long, oval to elliptic, paler on the undersides, stalks with very narrow or no wings. Flowers are 1–1.5cm (⅜–⅝in) wide and white. Fruits are a flattened globe shape with loose skin, bright orange, reaching 4cm (1½in) wide, produced on young plants (they make good marmalade).

CITRUS

Rutaceae

Origin: *S.E. Asia, Indonesia. A genus of 12 species of evergreen shrubs and trees which have been in cultivation for at least 2,000 years. Many are probably of hybrid origin and few can be found truly wild today. They are usually spiny plants with alternate, oval elliptic and oblong leaves which have a strong aroma when crushed and are*

borne on usually broadly winged stalks. Flowers are very fragrant and have white fleshy petals. They are borne in small corymbs and followed by large, leathery-skinned fruits (known botanically as a hesperidium) with juicy, segmented pulp. Citruses make good house and conservatory plants and can be raised from pips as fun plants. For the best fruits, however, named cultivars should be grown. Propagate by seed or by heel cuttings in summer, the latter method for cultivars.

Species cultivated

C. limon *(C. limonia, C. limonium)* Lemon S.E. Asia
A large shrub or small tree of 3–6m (10–20ft). Leaves are elliptic-oval, toothed, 5–10cm (2–4in) long, stalk with no or only very narrow wings. Flowers are white, 4cm (1½in) or more across, opening from a pink to purplish bud. Fruit is oval, 5–10cm (2–4in) long, thin-skinned with acid juice. *C.l.* 'Variegata' has leaves irregularly edged with yellow and the fruits are also striped green and yellow, the markings becoming less obvious as they ripen.

C. limonia *(C. limonium)* See *C. limon.*

C. medica Citron S.W. Asia
A shrub growing to 3m (10ft) and bearing stout spines. Leaves are oval-oblong, toothed, 5–10cm (2–4in) in length with no wings on the stalks. Flowers are white, pink in bud, opening to 3.5cm (1⅓in) or more across. Fruits are 5–10cm (2–4in) long, oval, yellow when ripe, the skins thick and rough, the pulp sour with little juice. Grown mainly for ornament.

C. meyeri See *C. limon.*

Below *Citrus medica*
Bottom *Citrus limon* 'Variegata'

Clethra arborea

CLETHRA
Clethraceae

Origin: *America, E. Asia and Madeira. A genus of 68 species of deciduous and evergreen shrubs of which one makes a handsome pot or tub specimen for the conservatory or large room, eventually outgrowing its space, but amenable to pruning. Propagate by cuttings with a heel in late summer with bottom heat.* Clethra *derives from* klethra, *the Greek word for an alder tree, the two genera having some similarities in appearance.*

Species cultivated
C. arborea Lily-of-the-valley tree Madeira
A small evergreen tree reaching 8m (26ft) in the wild, but shrubby when grown in a pot. Leaves are lance-shaped, finely toothed, 7–15cm (2¾–6in) long, bright glossy green above, and paler beneath. Flowers are white, cup-shaped, hanging in racemes up to 15cm (6in) long, several together making panicles at the ends of the stems.

COELOGYNE
Orchidaceae

Origin: *W. China and India to Malaysia and the Pacific islands. A genus of almost 200 species of epiphytic orchids (that is, they grow perched on trees) with rounded to flask-shaped pseudobulbs, each usually with two very narrow to lance-shaped leathery leaves. The*

flowers, which are in racemes or borne singly, have spreading tepals and a prominent lip, which can be lobed and deeply keeled. All grow well in the conservatory and home provided that enough humidity can be given to them. Those with hanging flowers are best grown in a basket. Propagate by division. Coelogyne *derives from the Greek* koilos, *a hollow and* gyne, *female, alluding to the somewhat hollow stigma.*

Coelogyne cristata

Species cultivated

C. cristata Himalaya
Clustered, egg- to globe-shaped pseudobulbs becoming wrinkled with age, growing to 6cm (2½in) long. Leaves are very narrow and lance-shaped, reaching a length of 30cm (1ft), two growing to each pseudobulb. Flowers are 8–10cm (3–4in) wide, white with strongly waved tepals; the lip has five rich-yellow keels; they are borne on arching to hanging racemes, 15–30cm (6–12in) long, in both winter and spring.

COFFEA
Rubiaceae

Origin: *Tropics of the Old World, chiefly Africa. A genus of 40 species of evergreen shrubs with opposite pairs of lance- to egg-shaped leaves and tubular, white, starry flowers in axillary clusters, followed by fleshy, red, berry-like fruits. These contain two seeds – the coffee beans that are sold commercially. They are decorative houseplants grown for their foliage, though they are not successful where the atmosphere*

Coffea arabica

is too dry. In the conservatory they can be grown in tubs and will flower and fruit. Propagate by tip cuttings in summer with bottom heat, or by seed in spring. Coffea *derives from the Arabic* kahwah.

Species cultivated
C. arabica Arabian coffee
An evergreen tree, growing in the wild to 5m (16ft), and a shrub when grown in a pot or tub. Leaves are oval to elliptic, dark glossy green and prominently veined, reaching a length of 5–15cm (2–6in). Flowers are 1cm (⅜in) across, white with narrow petals, fragrant, in clusters of one to six in late summer. The fruits are up to 1.5cm (⅝in) long. *C.a.* 'Nana' is a more compact form and most suitable for growing in the home.

CONVALLARIA
Liliaceae

Origin: *Northern temperate zones. A genus of one species of herbaceous perennial with a rhizomatous root system, cultivated as a pot plant for its strongly fragrant white flowers. It can be forced into bloom from December onwards. The traditional method is to dig up crowns in the autumn, ideally ones specially grown for this purpose and kept well manured for two years to give strong plants. Choose the one with the fattest buds with 10–15cm (4–6in) of rhizome. Place these about 5cm (2in) apart upright in 10–15cm (4–6in) pots of a peat compost and keep in a warm place at 16–24°C (60–75°F), ideally in a propagating frame with bottom heat. Batches treated in this way can be brought in at regular intervals of 1–2 weeks to provide a succession. The easiest method is to purchase specially prepared (low-temperature treated) crowns. These will force into growth and bloom at temperatures of 10–13°C (50–55°F) night minimum. Flowers can be had in 4–6 weeks.* Convallaria *derives from the Latin* convallis, *a valley, indicating that in the wild they often grow in valley or lowland woods.*

Convallaria majalis

Species cultivated

C. majalis (including *C. montana*) Lily-of-the-valley
This is a rhizomatous plant. The deep green leaves grow in pairs or threes, elliptic to lance-shaped, 15–20cm (6–8in) long. Flowers are waxy-white, strongly fragrant, roundly bell-shaped and nodding; they are borne in one-sided racemes equalling or shorter than the leaves. The fruits are orange-red berries. *C.m.* 'Aureo Variegata' has yellow longitudinal stripes on the leaves. *C.m.* 'Major', 'Fortin's Giant' and 'Berlin Giant' have larger flowers on long stems. *C.m.* 'Prolificans', ('Flore Pleno') has double flowers. *C.m.* 'Rosea' has pink flowers and is less strong growing.

CORONILLA

Leguminosae

Origin: *Europe, especially the Mediterranean region, Western Asia and the Canary Islands. A genus of 20 species of perennials, shrubs and sub-shrubs with alternate pinnate leaves. They have umbels of pea flowers followed by slender pods that are constricted between the seed (lomenta). Propagate by seed in spring or by cuttings with a heel in late summer.* Coronilla *is a diminutive form of the Latin* corona, *a crown; the umbels of flowers are often circular.*

Species cultivated

C. glauca See *C. valentina glauca*.
C. valentina Mediterranean region, S. Portugal
An evergreen shrub, up to 1–1.5m (3–5ft) tall. Leaves are bright green above, blue-green beneath, made up of seven to 15 notched leaflets, each to 2cm (¾in) long. The yellow flowers are 7–12mm (¼–½in) long, with a fragrance reminiscent of ripe peaches, and borne in five-to 12-flowered umbels in late spring and summer.
C. v. glauca (*C. glauca*)
Differs in having leaves that are blue-green on both surfaces. It will flower intermittently through the year.

Coronilla valentina glauca

Cymbidium lowianum

CYMBIDIUM
Orchidaceae

Origin: *Tropical Asia and Australia, often in montane forestlands. A genus of 40 species of orchid, including those that grow perched on a tree (epiphytes) and those that grow on the ground (terrestrial). They are clump-forming with usually egg-shaped to conical pseudobulbs. The bases of the very narrow, arching leaves sheathe the pseudobulbs. Flowers are rarely solitary, more usually borne in arching to hanging racemes. They have spreading, elliptic tepals and a prominent three-lobed lip in a contrasting colour. Cymbidiums are suitable for the warm conservatory or home and several are tolerant of short spells at lower temperatures. For home cultivation, however, the species have been largely superseded by their hybrids, which are numbered in thousands, new cultivars being produced every year. Among them is a strain of dwarf plants with upright flower spikes suitable for growing on a windowsill and these are now the main target of orchid breeders. Only the species are described here, as annually produced orchid catalogues can be referred to for the latest cultivars. Propagate by division.* Cymbidium *derives from the Greek* kymbe, *a boat, referring to the hollow, supposedly boat-like shape in the lip.*

Species cultivated
C. eburneum Himalaya from Sikkim to Burma
A ground-based species with small pseudobulbs hidden by the leaf bases. Leaves are narrowly sword-shaped to very narrow, bright green, growing to 60cm (2ft) long and 1.5cm (½in) wide. Racemes are erect, 30cm (1ft) long, carrying one to three flowers; each bloom

is 7–10cm (2¾–4in) wide, white to ivory, the lip marked with yellow; they are fragrant and open in late winter and spring.

C. e. parishii (*C. parishii*)
Shorter, broader leaves, growing to about 45cm (1½ft) long by 2.5cm (1in) wide, which are twice as wide as those of the type species, and stems with three to seven flowers.

C. lowianum Burma, Khasia Hills
Similar to *C. eburneum*, but smaller and with greenish-yellow flowers, the tepals cross-lined faintly with brownish red and the lip buff to yellow with a crimson central lobe, sometimes fragrant.

CYTISUS
Leguminosae

Origin: *Europe, Mediterranean region and North Atlantic islands. A genus of 30 species of deciduous and evergreen shrubs with alternate leaves, undivided or trifoliate, which may be short-lived, leaving green stems to carry out their functions. The flowers are typical of the pea family and the species described below is a good flowering shrub for the conservatory or windowsill and flowers freely when small. Propagate by seed in spring or by cuttings with a heel in late summer, preferably with bottom heat.* Cytisus *derives from the Greek* kytisos, *a name for several woody plants of the pea family.*

Species cultivated
C. × spachianus (*C. fragrans, C. racemosus, Teline × spachianus*)
A natural hybrid between *C. stenopetalus* and *C. canariensis* and often confused in gardens with the latter species. Leaves are trifoliate on stalks of 6mm (¼in); leaflets are oval, 1–2cm (⅜–¾in) long, green above, silky-hairy beneath. Flowers are rich yellow, growing to 12mm (½in) long, very fragrant, and borne in slender racemes 5–10cm (2–4in) long in winter and spring.

Cytisus × spachianus

DATURA
Solanaceae

Datura × candida 'Plena'

Origin: *Warm temperate regions, chiefly in Central America. A genus of 24 species of annuals, shrubs and trees, the shrubby members of which are sometimes included in* Brugmansia. *They are mainly poisonous, having alternate leaves and very large trumpet-shaped flowers opening to five spreading lobes. Daturas make free-flowering and beautifully fragrant shrubs for the conservatory or large room. Propagate by cuttings in late spring and summer.* Datura *is a Latin version of the Hindustani* dhatura, *or possibly of the Arabic* tatorah.

Species cultivated
D. × candida Angel's trumpet
Hybrid between *D. aurea* and *D. versicolor*. A tall shrub growing to 6m (20ft). Leaves are downy, oval to oblong-elliptic. Flowers are usually white, occasionally creamy-yellow or pink, 20–30cm (8–12in) long, the five lobes bent back and extended to 5–10cm (2–4in) long, and powerfully fragrant. Fruits are rarely seen. *D. × c.* 'Plena' (*D. × c.* 'Knightii', *D. knightii*) has double flowers, one inside the other.
D. cornigera
Confused with and in cultivation probably represented by *D. × candida*.
D. knightii See *D. × candida* 'Plena'.

DENDROBIUM
Orchidaceae

Dendrobium nobile

Origin: *Asia to Australasia and the Pacific Islands. A genus of 1,400 species of orchids that grow perched on trees (epiphytic), most of which have stem- or club-like pseudobulbs, lance-shaped leaves that are flat, or rolled under (never pleated) and the flowers in racemes. The blooms have spreading tepals and a lobed or smooth-edged lip, sometimes elaborately fringed. They are good pot plants for the conservatory and many will do well in the home; the evergreen sorts need only a short resting period, but the deciduous kinds must be given a cool, almost dry spell after flowering is completed. Propagate by division when re-potting, or by removing stem pseudobulbs and using as cuttings. Long pseudobulbs can be cut into two-noded sections.* Dendrobium *derives from the Greek* dendron, *a tree and* bios, *life, the plants being epiphytic.*

Species cultivated
D. densiflorum Himalaya to Burma
An evergreen plant. Pseudobulbs grow to 30–45cm (1–1½ft) tall, are

Dendrobium densiflorum

club-shaped and four-angled. Leaves are 15cm (6in), elliptic, deep glossy green, carried near the top of the pseudobulbs. Flowers are 5cm (2in) wide, tepals golden-yellow, with a velvety darker orange lip, not fringed; borne in long, dense, hanging racemes, to 22cm (9in) long, in spring.

D. nobile S.E. Asia from Himalaya to Taiwan

A semi-deciduous plant. Pseudobulbs grow to 60cm (2ft) tall, stem-like to narrowly club-shaped, upright. Leaves are 10cm (4in) long, oblong with notched tips. Flowers reach a width of 8cm (3in), not opening out fully, normally with white tepals tipped with pink; the lip white, red in the throat, but in some forms with richer-coloured flowers; fragrant and borne in clusters of one to three from the nodes of leafless pseudobulbs.

D. pierardii (*D. aphyllum*) S.E. Asia, Himalayas to Malaysia

A semi-deciduous plant. Pseudobulbs growing to 1–2m (3–6½ft) long, slender, hanging and stem-like. Leaves are up to 10cm (4in)

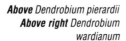

Above Dendrobium pierardii
Above right Dendrobium wardianum

long, pointed and lance-shaped. Flowers are 5cm (2in) wide, tepals white, lightly flushed with pink, often semi-transparent and fragile; the lip is yellow with purple streaking at the base; borne in clusters of one to three from the nodes of leafless pseudobulbs from late winter to late spring. Temperate.

D. wardianum S.E. Asia, Himalaya to Thailand
A deciduous plant. Pseudobulbs grow to 1m (3ft) or more tall, sturdy, stem-like, erect or arching. Leaves are 10cm (4in) long, narrowly lance-shaped shining green. Flowers are 9cm (3½in) wide, tepals white, tipped with reddish-purple; the lip hooded, marked with orange-yellow inside and two purple spots near the base, borne in clusters of one to three from the leafless pseudobulbs in spring. Temperate to tropical.

DISOCACTUS

Cactaceae

Disocactus nelsonii

Origin: *Northern South America, Central America, Mexico and West Indies. A genus of about seven species of cacti that grow perched on trees (that is, they are epiphytic) allied to* Epiphyllum. *They have slender, cylindrical main stems which bear flattened, leaf-like branches. The trumpet-shaped flowers appear from notches on the edges of these flattened stems. Suitable for the home and conservatory, these graceful cacti make good hanging basket subjects. Propagate by seed in spring or by cuttings in summer, using mature whole branches from the main stem or their tips.* Disocactus *derives from the Greek* dis, *twice,* isos *equal and* cactus, *referring to the two equal-numbered rows or rings of petals.*

Species cultivated

D. nelsonii (*Chiapasia nelsonii, Epiphyllum nelsonii*) South Mexico, Guatemala

Stems are at first erect, eventually arching to hanging, 60–120cm (2–4ft) in length; flattened side branches up to 25cm (10in) long by 3–4cm (1¼–1½in) wide. The rose-purple flowers grow to 10cm (4in) long by 6cm (2½in) wide, the petal tips are curved back, and supposedly violet-scented. A showy and free-flowering species.

DREGEA
Asclepiadaceae

Origin: *Tropical and South Africa to China. A genus of 12 species of climbing plants very closely related to Asclepias. Only one species is cultivated and this makes a very decorative plant for the conservatory or large room. Propagate by seed in spring or by cuttings in late summer.* Dregea *commemorates Johan Franz Drege (1794–1881), a German botanist who collected plants in South Africa.*

Dregea corrugata

Species cultivated
D. corrugata (*Wattakaka sinensis*) China
Stems are woody and twining, 2–3m (6½–10ft) in length. Leaves are more or less evergreen, or deciduous after long-term frost, in opposite pairs, oval with two lobes making a heart shape, to 10cm (4in) long, densely grey velvety downy beneath. Flowers are five-petalled with a small corona, white or cream with red speckling, 1.5cm (⅝in) wide, fragrant, borne in axillary, stalked umbels during the summer. In overall floral effect there is a strong resemblance to *Hoya*. Occasionally the intriguing seed pods form; these are paired, spindle-shaped follicles curved inwards, either smooth or corrugated and 5–7cm (2–2¾in) long. Fairly hardy.

DRIMYS
Winteraceae

Origin: *South America, Australasia to Borneo. A genus of 65 species of evergreen trees and shrubs with alternate leaves and five- to 20-petalled flowers in umbel-like clusters. They are followed by fleshy, berry-like fruits and make splendid foliage plants for the cool conservatory or large room with a bonus of attractive flowers when the plant is sufficiently mature. Propagate by cuttings with a heel in summer or by seed sown, if possible, as soon as ripe.* Drimys *is the Greek word for acrid, referring to the taste of the bark of* D. winteri *which can be used medicinally.*

Species cultivated
D. winteri (*Wintera aromatica*) Winter's bark
The name of a very varied species, in its broadest sense ranging from

Drimys winteri

Mexico south to Tierra del Fuego, but now considered to be correct only for plants from central Chile and adjacent Argentina. It makes a shrub in a container, and a tree reaching 5m (16ft) or more in the open garden in a mild climate. Leaves are oblong-elliptic, growing to 20cm (8in) long, glossy dark green, blue-green beneath. The fragrant flowers are 3–4cm (1¼–1½in) wide, with five to 20 creamy-white petals, borne in branched clusters in early summer.

EUCALYPTUS

Myrtaceae
Gum trees, Eucalypts

Origin: *Australia and Indo-Malaysia. A genus of about 500 species of evergreen trees and shrubs, many of which are colloquially known as gums. They have aromatic, leathery leaves and multi-stamened petalless flowers, which may be white, cream, yellow, pink or red. In most species the leaves of young plants (juvenile leaves) are borne in pairs and are a different shape from the adult ones. They are often more brightly hued, e.g. in the familiar blue gum, E. globulus, the juvenile leaves are oval with two lobes making a heart shape and blue-white in colour, whereas the adult ones are lance-shaped and more green than grey. The species described below make good tub or pot plants for conservatory and home when young. To retain juvenile foliage they must be cut back annually, or not less than every other year, in spring. Propagate by seed in spring. Eucalyptus derives from the Greek eu, well and kalypto, to cover; the united sepals and petals form a cap over the numerous showy stamens which is shed when the flower opens.*

Species cultivated
E. citriodora Lemon-scented gum Queensland
A tree growing to 45m (150ft) tall in the wild, but easily maintained

at under 2m (6½ft) with annual pruning. Juvenile leaves are oblong and lance-shaped, 8–15cm (3–6in) long, rough-textured and hairy; adult leaves are similar, but smooth; both are fragrant of oil of citronella when bruised. Flowers are white, but not borne on cut-back specimens.

E. globulus (*Tasmanian*) Blue gum Tasmania and Victoria
A large tree in the wild or planted out, but easily maintained at about 2m (6½ft) in containers. Juvenile leaves are oval with twin lobes making a heart shape, 8–15cm (3–6in) long, brightly blue-green; adult leaves are lance- to sickle-shaped, 13–30cm (5–12in) long, greyish-green. The creamy-white flowers are not borne on cut-back specimens. This is the easiest eucalypt to grow in a container, the juvenile phase being the most decorative.

E. nitens Shining gum Victoria
A large tree in the wild, but easily kept to 2m (6½ft) or so in a container. Young stems are square in cross-section, the angles with prominent, red-edged, crimped wings. Juvenile leaves grow to about 13cm (5in) long, oblong-oval with two lobes making a heart shape, blue-green, with a red mid-vein; lustrous green adult leaves reach a length of up to 20cm (8in), and are lance-shaped. Flowers are white, but not borne on cut-back plants in containers. Although not well known at present, this species rivals *E. globulus* as a decorative foliage plant when young and is worthwhile seeking out. It will stand several degrees of frost.

Eucalyptus nitens

EUCHARIS
Amaryllidaceae

Origin: *Tropical South America. A genus of about ten species of plants that grow from bulbs allied to* Hymenocallis. *Like that genus they have six-tepalled flowers with a central cup or corona formed of out-growths from the bases of the stamen filaments. The species described below thrive in containers and add a touch of class to a collection of flowering pot plants. Propagate by seed and offsets in spring.* Eucharis *derives from the Greek for charming, or pleasing.*

Species cultivated

E. grandiflora (*E. amazonica*) Amazon lily Colombia, Peru
These bulbs eventually form clumps. Leaves are evergreen and long-stalked; the blades are 20cm (8in) long, oblong to oval or elliptic, heavily textured and a lustrous deep green. Flowering stems are erect, 30–60cm (1–2ft) tall, topped by an umbel of three to six flowers; each bloom is like a narcissus, but with a slender curving tube. They are 8cm (3in) wide, white and fragrant. Summer is the usual flowering time, but if after each new flush of leaves has matured the plant is kept fairly dry for about six weeks, spring and autumn or winter flushes can be triggered off.

E. korsakovii

Eucharis korsakovii

This species is like a half-sized version of *E. grandiflora* which tolerates temperate conditions.

Eupatorium sordidum

EUPATORIUM
Compositae

Origin: *Mainly the Americas, but some also in Europe, Africa and Asia. A genus of about 1,200 species of shrubs and perennials grown for their abundant clusters of tiny groundsel-like flower heads. Among the frost-tender shrubs of this genus are several worthy of greater recognition as pot plants. Propagate by seed in spring or by cuttings in summer.* Eupatorium *honours Mithridates Eupator, King of Pontus, an ancient district of modern Turkey, who reputedly discovered that one species acted as an antidote to poison.*

Species cultivated
E. ianthinum See *E. sordidum.*

E. sordidum (*E. ianthinum*) Mexico

A shrub growing to 90cm (3ft) or more with fairly robust stems. Leaves are in opposite pairs, oval to broadly oblong, toothed, reaching a length of up to 10cm (4in) with longish stalks, deep green. Flowers are violet-purple, fragrant, growing in dense corymbose clusters up to 9cm (3½in) wide, mainly in winter. Temperate.

EUPHORBIA
Euphorbiaceae

Origin: *Cosmopolitan, though most frequent in sub-tropics and warm temperate regions. A genus of some 2,000 species of annuals, perennials and shrubs, many being succulent. Their foliage differs in almost every respect, but their flowers are remarkably alike. All have*

a cyathium – a small cup-shaped whorl of bracts which are fused together. This contains several male flowers each reduced to a single stamen, and one female flower which is no more than a three-lobed ovary. The bracts often bear crescent-shaped nectar glands, but sometimes have larger, petal-like structures. At the base of the cyathia are separate pairs of bracts called raylet leaves, and a ring of larger bracts called pseudumbel leaves at the base of each pseudumbel. These can be brightly coloured as in poinsettia. The fruits, which are three-lobed capsules, open explosively. The species described here is suitable for the conservatory and home, especially when small. The milky latex of most species of Euphorbia is highly irritant to eyes, mouth and tender skin. Propagate by seed, division where possible or by cuttings in summer. Euphorbia was supposedly named for Euphorbos, doctor to the king of Mauritania.

Species cultivated

E. mellifera Madeira, Canary Is.
A shrub reaching 2m (6½ft) in a pot, but in the wild up to 15m (48ft). Leaves are narrowly lance-shaped, mid- to dark green with a paler central vein; the raylet leaves are pale to reddish-brown. The cyathia are richly honey-scented, flowering in early spring.

Euphorbia mellifera

EXACUM
Gentianaceae

Origin: *Tropical Asia and India, islands of the Indian Ocean. A genus of 40 species of annuals, biennials and perennials with opposite, smooth-edged leaves and rounded flowers in clusters from the leaf axils. They are splendid flowering pot plants. Propagate by seed in spring, or for larger plants sow in autumn and these will flower earlier than spring-sown plants.* Exacum *derives from the Gaelic name* exacon, *a vernacular for* Centaurium *and used by Linnaeus for this genus.*

Exacum affine

Species cultivated
E. affine Socotra (Indian Ocean)
A bushy annual or biennial, 15–25cm (6–10in) tall. Leaves are broadly oval to elliptic, 1.5–4cm (⅝–1½in) long, shiny green. Flowers are 1.5–2cm (⅝–¾in) across, saucer-shaped, five-petalled, lavender-blue to purplish-blue, darker at the base of the petals, stamens yellow; they open from summer to autumn and are fragrant.

FORTUNELLA
Rutaceae
Kumquats

Origin: *Eastern Asia and the Malay Peninsula. A genus of four to six species of evergreen shrubs and small trees. They have undivided leaves, white flowers with five or more petals and orange-yellow to red fruits like those of small to miniature oranges. The species mentioned here provides a handsome, long-term pot plant, which is attractive at all times of the year. Propagate by seed when ripe or in spring, or by cuttings in summer.* Fortunella *honours Robert Fortune (1812–1880), a Scottish horticulturist, plant collector, traveller and author responsible for the establishment of the tea industry in India (from China) and the introducer to Britain of many now popular garden plants.*

Fortunella crassifolia
'Variegata'

Species cultivated
F. crassifolia Meiwa kumquat
Of unknown provenance, probably of hybrid origin and originating in China. A well-branched shrub, slightly thorny, 60–120cm (2–4ft) in height when grown in a pot. Leaves are 4–8cm (1½–3in) in length, oval, sometimes broadly so, thick-textured and deep green. Fruits are globular, 2.5–4cm (1–1½in) in diameter, orange, the thick rind sweet and edible. *F.c.* 'Variegata' has the leaves irregularly and heavily blotched with grey-green and cream.

FREESIA
Iridaceae

Origin: *South Africa. A genus of 20 species of deciduous perennials that grow from corms, with slender stems and narrow leaves mostly in fans growing from the plant base. The beautiful and colourful flowers are borne in one-sided spikes and face upwards. One species, together with the hybrids derived from it, is readily available, making splendid fragrant plants for the conservatory which can be brought into the home for flowering. They are also long-lasting cut flowers and are mostly grown for this purpose. For winter flowering, pot in September and for a succession of bloom, pot batches fortnightly until December, the last will open in spring. Water freely when growing and from the first appearance of the flowers until they finish give a fortnightly liquid feed. It is usually necessary to support the slender stems with canes and twine. Dry off when the leaves yellow in summer. Corms specially treated for the plant to flower in late summer can now be purchased. Propagate by separating offsets when re-potting, or by sowing seed in spring.* Freesia *was named for Frederick Freese* (d. 1876), *German doctor and a friend of the botanist who named the genus.*

Freesia × kewensis

Species cultivated
F. × kewensis (*F. × hybrida*)
A group of modern cultivars derived from crossing *F. armstrongii* with *F. refracta*. The flowers grow to 5cm (2in) long and are full, in a wide range of shades of red, mauve, pink, yellow, cream and white; there are also some double-flowered forms.

GARDENIA
Rubiaceae

Origin: *Warmer areas of Asia and Africa. A genus of 250 species of evergreen shrubs and trees with smooth-edged leaves in pairs or sometimes whorls of three or more. The flowers have five to 11 waxy petals, usually white or cream in colour. They are good conservatory plants and can be brought into the house at flowering time, but need good light and a humid atmosphere for success. Propagate by spring or summer cuttings with bottom heat.* Gardenia *was named for Dr Alexander Garden* (1730–1791), *a physician and naturalist of Scottish origin who lived in Charleston, S. Carolina, USA, and who corresponded with Linnaeus.*

Species cultivated
G. citriodora See *Mitriostigma axillare.*

G. jasminoides (*G. florida*, *G. grandiflora*) Common gardenia, Cape jasmine S. China
A shrub growing to 60cm (2ft) or more as a pot plant, and up to 2m (6½ft) in the open. Leaves are up to 10cm (4in) long, lance-shaped to oval, deep shining green, in whorls of three. Flowers reach 8cm (3in) across, are white and beautifully fragrant, borne in summer and autumn. The rarely seen wild form has five petals. *G.j. fortuniana* has larger, double flowers and is the sort usually seen in cultivation; 'Veitchiana' is winter-flowering, needing higher temperatures to flower (tropical); 'Prostrata' is a low-growing form with smaller leaves, sometimes listed as *G. radicans*.

G. taitensis Society and adjacent Pacific Islands
Much like *G. jasminoides*, but with single, scented blooms composed of five to nine radiating petals.

G. thunbergia South Africa
This evergreen shrub with whitish stems can eventually exceed 2m (6½ft) in height, but is easily kept down to half this. Leaves are elliptic, sometimes broadly so, 10–15cm (4–6in) long and a lustrous rich green. Flowers are usually eight-petalled, fragrant, white, 8cm (3in) or more wide, opening from winter to spring.

Gardenia jasminoides

HEBE

Scrophulariaceae

Origin: *Mainly New Zealand, also S.E. Australia, Tasmania, New Guinea, southern South America, Falkland Is. A genus of about 100 species of evergreen shrubs or occasionally small trees which have opposite pairs of smooth-edged leaves and racemes or panicles of small tubular flowers which open to four lobes. The species described below makes an attractive shrub for the conservatory, smaller ones making pretty, short-term houseplants. Propagate by cuttings of non-flowering shoots. Because of the ease with which they hybridize, seedlings are rarely true to type. Hebe was named for the Greek goddess of youth, cup-bearer to the gods and who married Hercules.*

Hebe diosmifolia

Species cultivated

H. diosmifolia New Zealand (North Island)

A shrub 60–150cm (2–5ft) tall, occasionally more in the wild. Leaves are 1.5–2.5cm (⅝–1in) long, lance-shaped to oval, dark green above, paler beneath, on hairy stalks. Flowers are lavender-blue to white, fragrant, carried in dense racemes up to 4cm (1½in) long, from the upper leaf axils; very free-flowering. Two forms appear to be available, the small one described here being an excellent pot plant.

HELIOTROPIUM

Boraginaceae

Heliotropium arborescens
'Marine'

Origin: *Tropics to warm temperate regions. A genus of about 250 species of annuals, shrubs and sub-shrubs with usually alternate, smooth-edged leaves and very fragrant flowers in one-sided cymes. The species described below is a good pot plant for the conservatory and can be brought indoors to a sunny windowsill. Propagate by cuttings from young shoots in spring or mature growth in late summer, also by seeds in late winter. Heliotropium derives from the Greek* helios, *sun and* trope, *turning, an allusion to the fallacy that the flowers turn to face the sun.*

Species cultivated

H. arborescens (*H. peruvianum*) Common heliotrope Peru

A shrub eventually growing to 2m (6½ft) or more. Leaves are 2.5–8cm (1–3in) long, lance-shaped, deep green with very conspicuous veining. Flowers are 6mm (¼in) long, purple to lavender, also white, in dense cymes, to 7cm (2¾in) long. A number of cultivars are grown, some more dwarf in habit, some of varying shades of purple. Not all are strongly fragrant.

HOMERIA

Iridaceae

Origin: *South Africa. A genus of about 40 species of plants which grow from corms, cultivated for their elegant and colourful blooms. They have solitary or sparse tufts of sword-shaped leaves and widely expanded, six-petalled flowers in loose branching clusters. Each flower lasts less than a day, but several to many buds open in succession. Propagate by seed in spring or by offsets when dormant. Re-pot annually in autumn or early spring. Best in the conservatory, but can be brought indoors when in bloom. Homeria derives from the Greek* homereo, *to meet, referring to the stamen filaments, which are joined together to form a tube. Not commemorating the Greek poet* Homer *as sometimes stated.*

Species cultivated

H. collina (*H. breyniana*) Cape tulip
The leaves grow two to four per corm, to about 60cm (2ft) in length when mature, very narrow, arching to recurved. Flowering stems are erect, about 45cm (1½ft) in height, the tips bearing slender, pointed, spindle-shaped green bracts which shelter the flower buds; flowers grow to 5cm (2in) or more wide, fragrant, in shades of pink, yellow or cream, borne in summer. *H.b.* 'Aurantiaca' has pink petals with a narrow basal blotch.

Homeria collina 'Aurantiaca'

HOYA

Asclepiadaceae

Origin: *S.E. Asia and the Pacific Islands. A genus of 200 species of evergreen climbers, some epiphytic (that is, growing perched on trees) with opposite pairs of fleshy, smooth-edged leaves and waxy, five-petalled flowers in large, hanging umbels. They are good house and conservatory plants, the climbers needing a support of canes or wires, the more shrubby sorts, particularly* H. bella, *being best in a hanging basket. Propagate by cuttings in warmth in summer. Hoya was named for Thomas Hoy (d. 1809), Head Gardener to the Duke of Northumberland at Syon House, Isleworth.*

Species cultivated

H. australis Australia (Queensland, New South Wales), New Guinea
A climber growing to 5m (16ft) or so, but less in containers. Leaves are rounded to broadly oval, about 8cm (3in) long, firmly fleshy, rich green. Flowers are fragrant, about 1.2cm (½in) wide, white with five red-purple spots in the centre, up to 50 in each umbel, opening in summer. Tropical.

Below left Hoya australis
Below Hoya bella

H. bella Miniature wax plant India

An epiphytic, branching shrub reaching a height of 45cm (1½ft), with arching to hanging stems. Leaves are up to 3cm (1¼in) long, oval to lance-shaped. Flowers are 1cm (⅜in) wide, white with a red centre, in umbels of eight to ten, opening in summer. Tropical.

H. carnosa Wax plant S. China to northern Australia

A climber growing to 6m (20ft) or more. Leaves are 5–8cm (2–3in), oval. Flowers are 1.5cm (⅝in) wide, white ageing to pink with a pink centre; they are very fragrant, especially at night, and are borne in large umbels from late spring to autumn, the same umbel often producing several flushes of bloom. *H.c.* 'Variegata' has cream-edged leaves. Temperate.

HYACINTHUS

Liliaceae
Hyacinth

Hyacinthus orientalis
'Pink Pearl'

Origin: *Central and eastern Mediterranean. A genus now considered to contain only one species, others once classified here now being included in* Brimeura, Bellevalia, Hyacinthella *and* Pseudomuscari. *It is a species which grows from bulbs from which many robust cultivars have been bred, with denser spikes of flowers and in a range of colours. They are favourite late winter-blooming plants for the home and conservatory. Pot the bulbs as soon as received, keep in a cool place until a good root system has been built up and the shoots are approaching 5cm (2in) tall, then bring into a warm room, but in a temperature not above about 16°C (61°F) for good growth and*

flowers. Propagate by removing offsets when dormant. Seed can be sown, but the resulting plants are rarely as good as their parents. Hyacinthus derives from an early pre-Greek language in which hyakinthos *denoted blue, and not, it is now believed, from the youth of that name who was accidentally killed by Apollo with a discus.*

Species cultivated

H. orientalis Common hyacinth
Leaves are 25–35cm (10–14in) long, strap-shaped, fleshy, deeply channelled, reaching to 2.5cm (1in) or more in width. Flowers are 2–3cm (¾–1¼in) long, bell-shaped, the six tepals widely spreading to recurved at the mouth, very fragrant, borne in a floppy to stiff raceme on 20–30cm (8–12in) tall stems in late winter to spring. Represented in cultivation by many named cultivars (Dutch hyacinths), including: 'City of Haarlem', yellow flowers; 'Delft's Blue', dark blue; 'Innocence', the best white; 'Lord Balfour', looser racemes, but of an almost magenta-pink; 'Orange Boven', an unusual shade of apricot; and 'Pink Pearl', bright, clear pink.

H.o. albulus Roman hyacinth
Smaller stems and flowers, with several flowering stems rising from each bulb. It is nearer to the original wild type and is found in southern France.

HYMENOCALLIS

Amaryllidaceae
Spider lilies

Origin: *Southern USA, Central and South America. A genus of about 30 species of plants which grow from bulbs, with strap-shaped leaves and six-tepalled flowers like yellow or white spidery daffodils. They are borne in umbels at the end of erect, leafless flowering stems. Plants are best in a conservatory and brought into the home only when flowering. Deciduous species must be kept barely moist once the leaves begin to yellow and until new leaves are well developed in spring.* Hymenocallis *derives from the Greek* hymen, *a membrane and* kallos, *beauty, referring to the corona, which is made up of joined membraneous outgrowths from the stamens.*

Hymenocallis littoralis

Species cultivated

H. calathina See *H. narcissiflora.*

H. × festalis (*Ismene × festalis*)
Hybrid between *H. longipetala* and *H. narcissiflora*, very like the latter, but with longer stamens.

H. littoralis (*H. americana; H. senegambica* in part) Tropical America, naturalized in West Africa
Leaves are evergreen, strap-shaped, widely arching, growing up to

Hymenocallis narcissiflora

90cm (3ft) long, bright green. Flowering stems are 45–75cm (1½–2½ft) tall, bearing four to eight or more white flowers; each bloom has a green-flushed tube about 15cm (6in) long, a funnel-shaped corona to 5cm (2in) and six linear petals 8–13cm (3–5in) in length. Late spring to summer is the flowering season.

H. narcissiflora (*H. calathina*) Basket flower, Peruvian daffodil
Peru, Bolivia

Leaves reach 60cm (2ft) long. Flowering stems also grow to 60cm (2ft) tall, carrying blooms with a 5cm (2in) long corona from which the stamens project a further 2.5cm (1in). The flowers open in spring and summer.

JASMINUM

Oleaceae
Jasmines

Origin: *Asia, Africa and Australia, mostly from tropical regions. A genus of 200 to 300 species of deciduous and evergreen shrubs. They have opposite pairs of leaves which can be pinnate, trifoliate or undivided. The flowers are tubular with six (rarely from four to nine) petal-like lobes opening flat at the mouth and followed by black berries. Plants are suitable for the conservatory or a home windowsill where they can be trained on wires or canes. Propagate by cuttings in late summer. Jasminum was derived from the Arabic name Yasmin for this genus.*

Species cultivated

J. officinale Common white/Summer jasmine, Poet's jessamine
Caucasus to Western China

A vigorous deciduous twiner growing up to 4m (13ft) in a pot, and reaching 10m (33ft) in the open, with green stems. The leaves are trifoliate, the leaflets 1.5–2.5cm (⅝–1in) long, oval, the end one tapering to a slender point. The white flowers are about 2cm (¾in) across, very fragrant, and carried in clusters at the ends of the stems from summer into autumn. *J.o. affine* has pink-tinged buds; 'Aureovariegatum' has the leaves and shoots irregularly blotched with yellow.

J. polyanthum Pink jasmine, Chinese jasmine Western China
An evergreen or partly deciduous twiner growing to 3m (10ft) or more. Leaves are pinnate, the leaflet at the end being slender-pointed. Flowers are 2cm (¾in) wide, white, pink when in bud. They are brightest in good light, very fragrant and borne in abundance in spring and summer.

Jasminum polyanthum

LAELIA
Orchidaceae

Origin: *Mexico to tropical South America. A genus of 30 species of epiphytic orchids (that is, they grow perched on trees) closely allied to* Cattleya *and separated by the number of pollinia (not a true anther, but looking like several stamens fused together) to each flower,* Cattleya *having four,* Laelia *eight. They are best in the conservatory but can be grown in the home. Propagate by division in spring or after blooming.* Laelia *was named after one of the Vestal Virgins.*

Species cultivated
L. anceps Mexico to Belize
Pseudobulbs reaching a height of 7–15cm (2¾–6in), oblong-oval, flattened, either clustered or spaced apart on stout, creeping

Laelia anceps

rhizomes. Leaves are 15–23cm (6–9¼in) long, oblong lance-shaped, one from each pseudobulb. Flowers are sometimes fragrant, growing to 10cm (4in) wide, the tepals lilac-pink with a yellow-striped and purple-edged lip; two to five blooms are carried together on 60–90cm (2–3ft) long racemes. Many forms and cultivars have been described.

LAURUS

Lauraceae
Laurels

Laurus nobilis

Origin: *Mediterranean region and North Atlantic islands. A genus of two species of evergreen trees of which one is commonly grown both as a decorative foliage plant and for its leaves, which are used as a flavouring in cooking. It makes an excellent pot or tub plant and can be pruned or cut back if it gets too large for its situation. For a sturdy plant, standing outside in summer is recommended. Propagate by cuttings in summer, or by seed. Laurus is the Latin name of this plant.*

Species cultivated
L. nobilis Bay, Sweet bay Mediterranean region
Growing to 10–20m (32–65ft) in the wild, but easily kept to 1.2m (4ft) in a pot. Leaves are 5–8.5cm (2–3½in) long, narrowly oval to oval, leathery, glossy deep green and strongly aromatic when crushed. Flowers are unisexual, produced in axillary clusters in spring. Fruits are a black egg-shaped, berry-like drupe, 1–1.5cm (⅜–⅝in) long. Hardy. *L.n.* 'Aurea' has golden-tinted foliage.

LILIUM

Liliaceae
Lilies

Origin: *Northern hemisphere. A genus of about 80 species of perennial plants with bulbs made up of a number of separate overlapping scales. They have erect stems with narrow leaves and racemes of colourful flowers which can be trumpet-, funnel-, star-, bowl- or Turk's-cap-shaped. With the exception of the Easter lily (L. longiflorum), many species and cultivars are reasonably frost-hardy and usually thought of as plants for the open garden. However, almost all lilies also grow well in pots and, depending upon the available warmth, will bloom well ahead of their usual season in the unheated, cool, or temperate conservatory. When in bloom they can be brought into the home. Any standard compost is suitable and 20–30cm (8–12in) pots the best sizes, though single bulbs can be grown in 15cm (6in) containers. Place the stem-rooting species in the bottom third of the pot so that at least 10cm (4in) of compost is above*

Lilium formosanum

the nose of the bulb. After blooming, place the containers outside in a sheltered site. If kept well fed and re-potted annually in autumn they will flower as regularly as any more orthodox pot plants. Propagate by separating bulblets when potting, by sowing stem bulbils (miniature bulbs) in late summer, removing bulb scales in winter or, with the species only, sowing seed in spring. Lilium *is a form of the Latin common name for the Madonna lily.*

Species cultivated

L. formosanum (*L. philippinense formosanum, L. longiflorum formosanum*) Taiwan
Stems are 1–1.4m (3–4½ft) tall. The dark green leaves grow to 20cm (8in) long, very narrow, along the length of the stem, densest on the lower parts. Flowers are 13–20cm (5–8in) long, funnel-shaped, white, marked outside with chocolate to purple, fragrant; they open in summer and autumn.

L. longiflorum Easter/White trumpet lily Japan
Stems grow to a height of 90cm (3ft), with leaves up to 18cm (7in) long, lance-shaped, pointed and glossy-green. Flowers are 13–18cm (5–7in) long, pure white, fragrant, opening throughout the summer.

LIPPIA
Verbenaceae

Lippia citriodora

Origin: *North and South America, Africa. A genus of 200 species of shrubs and perennials with smooth-edged leaves and spikes or panicles of small, tubular flowers. The species described below is best in a conservatory, though it can be grown in a sunny window where it can be cut back hard in spring to keep it small and tidy. Propagate by cuttings in either spring or summer or by seed sown in spring. Lippia was named for Augustin Lippi (1678–1701), an Italian botanist killed in Ethiopia while plant collecting.*

Species cultivated
L. citriodora (*Aloysia citriodora, Verbena triphylla*) Lemon verbena Argentina, Chile

A deciduous shrub rarely more than 90cm (3ft) in a pot if cut back annually; growing to 3m (10ft) in the open garden. Leaves are 6–10cm (2½–4in) long, in opposite pairs, or whorls of three, lance-shaped, strongly lemon-scented (the source of verbena oil). Flowers are very small, two-lipped, white or very pale purple, borne in axillary spikes or panicles at the ends of the stems in late summer and autumn.

MANDEVILLA
Apocynaceae

Mandevilla boliviensis

Origin: *Central and South America. A genus of 100 species of woody climbers often still grown under the name* Dipladenia. *They have smooth-edged leaves in whorls or opposite pairs, and racemes of funnel-shaped blooms opening to five spreading lobes, twisted in bud. They do well in large pots or tubs and are best in a conservatory, but can be tried in a large room. Propagate by seed in spring, or by cuttings of short shoots growing off the main stem in summer with bottom heat. Mandevilla was named for Henry John Mandeville, British Minister in Argentina and the introducer of the first species into cultivation.*

Species cultivated
M. boliviensis Bolivia

Climbing to 3m (10ft) or more, but can be kept smaller. Leaves are 5–8cm (2–3in) long, oblong, slender-pointed, shining green. Flowers grow to 5cm (2in) wide, the petal lobes slightly twisted, white with a golden-yellow eye.

M. laxa (*M. suaveolens*) Chilean jasmine Peru, Bolivia, Argentina

A vigorous twiner growing to 5m (16ft) or more. Leaves are up to 10cm (4in) long, oblong-oval with two lobes making a heart shape,

Above Mandevilla laxa
Left Mandevilla splendens

with a slender point. Flowers grow to 5.5cm (2¼in) long, white and fragrant, in clusters of five to 15, opening in summer.

M. splendens Brazil

Up to 3m (10ft) in height with leaves growing to 20cm (8in) long, broadly elliptic, thinner in texture, shining green. Flowers are 10cm (4in) or more across, white and flushed with rose-pink.

M. suaveolens See *M. laxa*.

MATTHIOLA

Cruciferae

Origin: *Azores and Canary Islands westwards through the Mediterranean region to central Asia. A genus of 55 species of annuals, biennials, perennials and shrubs, with leaves borne alternately or in rosettes, usually undivided but sometimes pinnatifid. The species described below makes an excellent pot plant which can be grown in the conservatory and brought into a cool room for flowering. Propagate by seed in spring for summer blooms; sow in late summer to flower the following winter and spring and provide temperate conditons. Matthiola was named for Pierandrea Mattioli (1500–1577), an Italian doctor and botanist.*

Species cultivated

M. incana Stock S.W. Europe on coasts

A woody-based perennial 30–80cm (12–32in) tall, normally grown as

Matthiola incana
Brompton strain

an annual or biennial. Leaves are 5–10cm (2–4in) long, very narrow to oblong lance-shaped, covered with grey-white felt. Flowers are 2–3cm (¾–1¼in) across, purple, pink or white. In cultivation, red, purple-blue and yellow colours occur and the following strains are used: Ten-week stocks, and Brompton or East Lothian stocks. Ten-week stocks are treated as annuals and are up to 30cm (1ft) tall, branched, with single flowers. Also similar are Trysomic, which have 85% double flowers, and All Double with 100% doubles. When these are in the seedling stage it is possible to identify and discard the single-flowered plants as they are much greener than the somewhat yellowish doubles. Column and Excelsior strains grow to 90cm (3ft) and are good for cutting, but make less satisfactory pot plants. Brompton stocks are grown as biennials and reach 45cm (1½ft) in height; they are well-branched plants and the flowers can be single or double. East Lothian stocks are shorter, reaching about 37cm (15in), and can be grown as annuals or biennials.

MAXILLARIA
Orchidaceae

Origin: *The Americas from Florida to Argentina. A genus of about 300 species of mainly epiphytic orchids (that is, they grow perched on trees). Most have conspicuous pseudobulbs and tend to form clumps*

and grow from rhizomes. Their leaves are very narrow to elliptic and the flowers solitary, composed of five spreading tepals and a deeply three-lobed lip. These orchids are suitable for growing in pots or pans or attached to pieces of bark. Propagate by division when re-potting in spring. Maxillaria derives from the Latin maxilla, a jaw, the flowers supposedly resembling the jaws of an insect.

Maxillaria picta

Species cultivated

M. picta Brazil
These pseudobulbs are clustered or spaced along the rhizomes, and are 5–8cm (2–3in) tall, egg-shaped. Leaves grow one or two together, to 30cm (1ft) or more long, narrowly oblong and glossy green. Flowers are 6cm (2½in) wide, creamy-white in colour, heavily spotted and dotted with purple, the lip white with purple markings, opening in winter and spring.

MITRIOSTIGMA
Rubiaceae

Origin: *Tropical and southern Africa. A genus of three species of evergreen shrubs related to* Gardenia. *One species has long been grown in greenhouses and makes a pleasing pot plant for the home, flowering when quite small. Propagate by cuttings in spring or summer.*

Mitriostigma axillare

Mitriostigma *derives from the Greek* mitra, *a mitre, and* stigma, *the pollen-receptive organ attached to the ovary within a flower.*

Species cultivated

M. axillare (*Gardenia citriodora*) Wild coffee South Africa, Natal
A well-branched spreading shrub, in the wild reaching 1.5m (5ft) tall, but easily kept to half this in containers. Leaves grow in opposite pairs, are 5–10cm (2–4in) long, lance-shaped to narrowly elliptic, leathery-textured, usually dark glossy green, somewhat wavy. Flowers are 1.2cm (½in) wide with a tubular base and five rounded lobes, white, with the scent of orange blossom, borne in small clusters from the leaf axils in spring. In general appearance this species is more like *Coffea* than *Gardenia*.

MONSTERA
Araceae

Origin: *Tropical America. A genus of 25 species of evergreen root climbers plants which in the wild climb trees with aerial roots. They have alternate, long-stalked leaves which can be oval to oblong, and tiny petalless flowers carried on a spadix within a spathe typical of*

Monstera deliciosa 'Variegata'

members of the arum family. They are familiar pot plants in conservatory or home, tolerant of poor light and a dry atmosphere, but looking much more healthy and attractive where humidity is provided. They grow particularly well on a moss stick. Propagate by stem tip or leaf bud cuttings in warmth in summer. Monstera may be derived from the Latin monstrifer, monster-bearing, referring to its large, oddly perforated leaves, but this is by no means certain.

Species cultivated

M. deliciosa (*M. pertusa, Philodendron pertusum*) Ceriman, Swiss cheese plant, Mexican bread fruit Mexico to Central America
A very tall climber in warm countries, but rarely reaching more than 2–3m (6–10ft) in a pot. Leaves are 40–90cm (16–36in) long, broadly oval with deeply cleft edges, leaving curved, blunt-ended oblong lobes; on mature plants they are also perforated with large elliptic to oblong holes. Spathes grow to 20cm (8in) or more long, are creamy-white or green. Fruits are egg-shaped, with a pineapple-like scent; they are edible but contain minute spicules which can prove an irritant to sensitive throats. *M.d.* 'Variegata' has variable yellowish-green markings, but is unstable and very liable to revert to a dark green colour.

MYRTUS

Myrtaceae
Myrtles

Origin: *Tropics and sub-tropics. A genus of 100 species of evergreen shrubs and trees with smooth-edged, lance-shaped to oval leaves carried in opposite pairs, and four- to five-petalled flowers followed by fleshy berries which in many species are edible. They make decorative pot plants. Propagate by seed in spring, or by heel cuttings in summer. Myrtus is the Greek common name for this genus.*

Myrtus communis

Species cultivated

M. communis Common myrtle W. Asia

A shrub growing to 2m (6½ft) in a pot; up to twice this in the open. Leaves are 2.5–5cm (1–2in) long, lance-shaped to oval, glossy rich green. Flowers are 2cm (¾in) wide, white, fragrant, borne singly in summer and followed by 9–12mm (⅓–½in) long purple-black berries. *M.c.* 'Microphylla' is lower growing, with leaves to 2cm (¾in) long; 'Variegata' has the leaves edged with creamy-white.

PANCRATIUM

Amaryllidaceae

Origin: *Mediterranean region to tropical Africa and Asia. A genus of about 15 species of perennials which grow from bulbs with strap-shaped leaves growing from the plant base, and umbels of somewhat daffodil-like flowers on long, leafless stems. The blooms are white and funnel-shaped, opening to six narrow, spreading lobes and within these a corona made up of the widened, joined stamen bases, the upper part of the stamens remaining free. They are suitable both for the conservatory or for flowering in the home. Propagate by separating offsets, or by seed when ripe or in spring.* Pancratium *is from the Greek common name for a bulbous plant, though not necessarily of this genus.*

Pancratium illyricum

Species cultivated

P. illyricum Spain, Corsica, Sardinia

The leaves are deciduous, 45cm (1½ft) long, broadly strap-shaped, blue-green. Flowers are 8cm (3in) long, having a short corona, six to 12 blooms in each umbel, on smooth, cylindrical stems; very fragrant, opening in late spring.

PANDOREA

Bignoniaceae

Origin: *Malaysia to central Australia. A genus of eight species of evergreen, twining climbers with pinnate leaves in opposite pairs and axillary panicles of colourful funnel- to bell-shaped flowers opening to five spreading lobes. Although amenable to pruning, they will not flower so well if cut back hard. Propagate by summer cuttings in bottom heat, or by seed in spring in warmth.* Pandorea *was named for Pandora, in Greek mythology the first woman sent to earth by Zeus.*

Species cultivated

P. jasminoides Bower plant Australia

Growing to 5m (16ft) in a pot, much more in the open ground. Leaves

Pandorea jasminoides

have five to nine lance-shaped to oval leaflets, each 2.5–5cm (1–2in) long. Flowers are 3–5cm (1¼–2in) long and 5cm (2in) across, white with pink in the throat, in few-flowered panicles, opening from winter to summer. *P.j.* 'Alba' has pure white flowers; 'Rosea' is pink with a darker throat.

PELARGONIUM

Geraniaceae
Geraniums

Pelargonium cucullatum

Origin: *Widespread throughout warm temperate areas of the New World, concentrated in South Africa but also in north Africa and the adjacent Atlantic islands and eastwards to Arabia and southern India, also in Australasia; those listed below from South Africa unless stated. Long ago included in* Geranium *and still often sold under that name. A genus of 250 to 280 species mainly of shrubs and sub-shrubs, but including annuals and perennials, most of which are adapted to areas of low rainfall. Some are succulent or almost so. Their main characteristics are the five-petalled flowers, which have a small nectary spur joined to the stalk of the flower, and are carried in stalked, axillary umbels. The beaked fruit split open explosively when ripe. The species described below are all good house and conservatory plants, flowering in summer. Propagate by seed in spring or by cuttings taken in spring or summer.* Pelargonium *is derived from the Greek* pelargos, *a stork, an allusion to the long-beaked fruit.*

Species cultivated

P. capitatum Rose-scented geranium
Shrubby, with straggling, white-hairy stems growing prostrate with the tips upright, 30–60cm (1–2ft) tall. Leaves grow up to 5cm (2in) across, three- to five-lobed and toothed, softly hairy. Flowers are 2cm (¾in) long, pink with red-purple veins, carried in umbels of eight to 24 on slender stalks.

P. crispum Lemon geranium, Prince Rupert geranium
An erect, branched shrub reaching a height of 60–90cm (2–3ft).
Leaves are 2–3cm (¾–1in) wide, shallowly three-lobed, greyish, with
crisped or curled edges, borne close together in two ranks up the
stems and strongly lemon-scented. Flowers are 2–2.5cm (¾–1in)
long, white to pink with darker reddish veining, borne singly or in
twos or threes. *P.c.* 'Variegatum' has yellow-blotched leaves.

P. cucullatum
A freely-branched shrub up to 2m (6½ft) tall, softly hairy. Leaves
reach 6cm (2½in) across, kidney-shaped, more or less cupped with
finely scalloped or toothed edges. Flowers are 4–5cm (1½–2in)
across, purplish-red with darker veins. A pale purple sort is sometimes offered under this name and is a form or possibly a hybrid of
this species.

PERESKIA
Cactaceae

Origin: *Mexico, West Indies, Central and South America. A genus of
about 20 species of trees, shrubs and climbers often considered to be
like the ancestral stock from which the true cacti of today evolved.
Unlike most true cacti they have recognizable leaves, but bear areoles
within the leaf axils. Most have showy, many-petalled flowers and
fleshy fruits which are edible. The climbers need some support. Keep
almost dry from the time the leaves yellow in autumn until spring.
Propagate by cuttings in summer, or from seed in spring in heat.
Pereskia was named for Nicholas Claude Fabre de Peiresc (1580–
1637), a French naturalist.*

Pereskia aculeata

Species cultivated
P. aculeata Barbados gooseberry Mexico to Argentina
Shrubby at first, then sending up long, scrambling shoots to a height
of 10m (33ft) in the open; they have hooked spines on the climbing
stems arising from areoles. Leaves are 5–10cm (2–4in) long, lance-
shaped to elliptic, with prominent midribs. Flowers are 2.5–4cm
(1–1½in) wide, white, yellow or pale pink with a fragrance that is not
always thought pleasant; they are carried in panicles during autumn
and are followed by pale yellow fruits, spiny at first, but smooth
when ripe.

PHAIUS
Orchidaceae

Origin: *S.E. Asia to the Himalaya, Malagasy. A genus of 50 species of
orchids, most of which are ground dwelling. They have clustered*

Phaius tankervillae

pseudobulbs which can be short and thick or stem-like and leafy. Flower stems usually arise from the sides of the pseudobulbs and bear erect racemes of flowers with five similar tepals and a large, often trumpet-shaped lip. They are best in the conservatory, but can be brought into the house for short spells if extra humidity can be given. Propagate by division when repotting or by severing back bulbs in spring. Phaius *derives from the Greek* phaios, dark, *referring to the flower colour of the first species described.*

Species cultivated
P. tankervillae (*P. bicolor, P. blumei, P. grandiflorus, P. gravesii, P. wallichii*) Nun's hood Himalaya, S.E. Asia to northern Australia
A very variable orchid especially in its flower size and colour, hence the number of names that have been applied to different forms of it. They bear pseudobulbs which are 10cm (4in) tall and which are broadly egg-shaped. Leaves are 60–90cm (2–3ft) long, narrowly elliptic to oblong, pointed. Flowers reach 10–13cm (4–5in) across, tepals reddish brown edged with yellow inside and white on the back, the lip is trumpet-shaped, yellowish-brown inside with a red-purple throat patch; they are very fragrant and carried in racemes on stiffly erect stems 1m (3ft) or more in height.

PODRANEA
Bignoniaceae

Origin: *Tropical and South Africa. A genus of two species of woody-stemmed twining climbers, one of which is in cultivation though not very readily available. Best in a conservatory but can be tried in a large room. Propagate by cuttings in summer or by seed in spring.* Podranea *is an anagram of* Pandorea, *the genus to which it is most closely related and in which it was once included.*

Podranea ricasoliana

Species cultivated

P. ricasoliana (*Pandorea ricasoliana*) South Africa (Cape)
An evergreen climber reaching 4m (13ft) or more in length. Leaves grow in opposite pairs, are pinnate, composed of seven to nine (sometimes less or more) lance-shaped to oval leaflets each one about 5cm (2in) in length, wavy-edged and dark green. Flowers are 5cm (2in) long, tubular bell-shaped with five large rounded petal lobes, rose-pink, darker veined, fragrant, in loose panicles at the ends of the stems. This is a beautiful and free-flowering species deserving to be seen more often. Will stand slight frost and is then partially or wholly deciduous.

PRIMULA

Primulaceae

Origin: *World-wide, but mainly in the northern hemisphere and particularly Asia. A genus of about 400 species of evergreen and deciduous perennials which are tufted or clump-forming in habit. They have lance- to disc-shaped leaves in rosettes growing from the base of the plant and umbels of tubular flowers opening to five broad lobes carried on leafless stems (scapes). In some species the scape is so reduced that the individual stalks of the flowers which make up the umbel arise near the base of the plant and appear separate. The petals are usually oval and notched at the tip. Individual plants can have the stigma longer than the stamens (pin-eyed), or vice versa (thrum-eyed). Primulas suitable for growing in the conservatory or home fall into two groups. P. × tommasinii (polyanthus) is potted from late autumn onwards and will flower in about a month from being brought into warmth. It must be returned to the open garden after flowering. The tender species are full-time house and conservatory plants and, although short-lived perennials, are*

Below left Primula × tommasinii **Below** Primula malacoides

normally treated as annuals. They are sown from spring to late summer and will flower in winter and spring, 9–15 months later. Pot on regularly, the best plants being obtained from those in 13cm or 15cm pots. For winter flowering, plants require temperate conditions. Propagate by seed or by division of hardy species. Primula *derives from the Latin* primus, *first, referring to the early spring primrose.*

Species cultivated

P. malacoides Fairy primrose Western China.
Leaves grow to 7cm (2¾in) long, oval to oblong-elliptic, with two lobes at the leaf base making it heart-shaped, toothed, hairy beneath, on long stalks. Flowers are 1–2cm (⅜–¾in) across, fragrant, light mauve in the original species, with three to six whorls on the 30–45cm (1–1½ft) stems. Now represented in cultivation by forms with single or double flowers in shades of red, pink, purple and white. Dwarf forms 15–20cm (6–8in) tall are also available. Most are sold as colour mixes, but single colours are sometimes offered. Recommended forms are: 'Carmine Pearl', dwarf, carmine-red; 'Fire Chief', brick-red; 'Lilac Queen', soft lilac, double; 'Mars', deep lavender; and 'White Pearl', dwarf, white.

P. polyantha See *P.* × *tommasinii.*

P. × **tommasinii** Polyanthus
A hybrid between *P. veris* and coloured forms of *P. vulgaris.* Leaves grow up to 25cm (10in) long, oval, wrinkled and often downy beneath. Flowers grow to 2.5cm (1in) or more across, in umbels on stems 15cm (6in) or more long; they are available in shades of red, pink, purple, blue, yellow and white. 'Pacific' has very large flowers up to 5cm (2in) across.

SANSEVIERIA

Agavaceae (Liliaceae)
Snake plant

Origin: *Africa and southern Asia. A genus of about 60 species of succulent evergreen perennials some of which are ground-dwelling in the wild, others grow perched on trees (epiphytic). They have rosettes or clumps of rather stiff sword-shaped or cylindrical leaves and somewhat tubular flowers in axillary racemes or panicles followed by usually red berries. They are best left in the same pot until they have totally filled it before repotting. Propagate by division or by cuttings of leaf sections in summer.* Sansevieria *was named for Prince Raimond de Sanagrio de Sanseviero (1710–1771).*

Species cultivated

S. hyacinthoides *(S. guineensis, S. spicata, S. thyrsiflora)* South Africa

Sansevieria trifasciata

Leaves are lance-shaped, growing to 45cm (1½ft) in length, tapering to a grooved leaf stalk, dark green edged with yellow and with pale cross-bands. Flowers are fragrant, greenish-white, in racemes up to 75cm (2½ft) tall.

S. trifasciata Mother-in-law's tongue, Snake plant South Africa
A clump-forming plant. Leaves reach a length of 45cm (1½ft) in a container, twice this in the open ground, very narrowly lance-shaped, stiffly erect, deep green cross-banded with paler greens. Flowers grow up to 1.5cm (⅝in) long, are greenish-white and give off scent at night.

SELENICEREUS

Cactaceae
Night blooming sereus

Origin: *Southern USA to South America. A genus of about 20 species of epiphytic cacti (that is, they grow perched on trees) that flower at night. They have long ribbed stems which climb or trail and have aerial roots. Most species have spine-bearing areoles. The flowers are*

Selenicerus hamatus

usually very large and sweetly scented, mostly white in colour and followed by round, fleshy red fruits. These plants are easy to grow, but need space for their long stems, which can be trained on wires or allowed to sprawl through shrubs. Propagate by cuttings of stem sections 10–15cm (4–6in) long in summer. Selenicereus derives from the Greek selino, the moon and Cereus, the cactus genus, referring to its appearance and night flowering.

Species cultivated
S. hamatus Southern and eastern Mexico

A fast-growing species with slender, mainly four-ribbed stems growing to a length of 5m (15ft) if planted out in a conservatory border. The ribs, which usually number four, bear short, down-pointing spurs at about 5cm (2in) intervals; each spur has a brown areole and four to six bristle-like whitish spines. Flowers are 20–25cm (8–10in) long and almost as wide at the mouth, white to yellow, aromatically fragrant, and borne in summer and autumn.

SOLANDRA
Solanaceae

Origin: *Mexico and West Indies to tropical South America. A genus of about ten species of scrambling climbers much prized in tropical horticulture for their large, trumpet-shaped, fragrant flowers. They are robust plants with long, thrusting shoots and alternate undivided leaves. Those species described below make handsome pot or tub plants, but are seen to best effect when planted out in the conservatory. Solandra honours the Swedish Daniel Carl Solander (1736–1782), a pupil of Linnaeus, botanist on Captain Cook's first voyage to the Pacific (1768–1771) and later Keeper of the Natural History Department of the British Museum.*

Solandra maxima

Species cultivated

S. hartwegii See *S. maxima*.

S. maxima (*S. hartwegii*, *S. nitida*) Cup of Gold Mexico
A vigorous plant, with stems 5–10m (16–33ft) long. Leaves are smooth and hairless, elliptic, to 15cm (6in) long, usually deep green and lustrous. Flowers reach a length of 22cm (9in) and are yellow with five purple lines.

S. nitida See *S. maxima*.

STEPHANOTIS

Asclepiadaceae

Origin: *Malagasy, southern Asia east to Malaysia and Peru. A genus of about 15 species of woody climbers with opposite, undivided, usually leathery-textured leaves and jasmine-like tubular flowers opening to five spreading lobes. The species described below is a handsome pot plant, needing canes, wires or a trellis to support the long, twining shoots. Prune in winter before new growth is made. Propagate by seed or semi-hardwood cuttings in summer, both in heat, or by layering.* Stephanotis *derives from the Greek* stephanos, *crown and* otis, *ear, referring to the crown of stamens, which have outgrowths supposedly like ears.*

Species cultivated

S. floribunda Madagascar jasmine Malagasy
An evergreen climber that can be kept to 60cm (2ft) by twining around a low support, but is capable of reaching 5m (16ft) or more.

Stephanotis floribunda

Leaves grow in opposite pairs, 5–10cm (2–4in) long, broadly elliptic with a mucronate tip, glossy dark green. Flowers are about 4cm (1½in) long, white, waxy-textured and fragrant, borne in axillary cymes from spring to autumn.

TABERNAEMONTANA
Apocynaceae

Tabernaemontana divaricata

Origin: *Tropical Africa and Asia. A genus, depending upon the botanical authority, of 100 to 150 species of evergreen trees and shrubs. One species is widely planted in the tropics and makes a handsome tub plant for the warm conservatory. Propagate by cuttings in summer or by layering in spring.*

Tabernaemontana *honours Jakob Theodor von Bergzabern (d. 1590), who Latinized his name to* Tabernaemontanus *under which pseudonym he wrote the classic herbal* Neuw Kreuterbuch.

Species cultivated
T. divaricata (*T. coronaria, Ervatamia coronaria*) Cape jasmine, East Indian rosebay India

A well-branched shrub reaching 2m (6½ft) or more in height. Leaves grow in opposite pairs and are 8–15cm (3–6in) long, elliptic to lance-shaped or narrowly oval, and lustrous. Flowers form in small clusters, with a tubular base and five large, white, wavy petals up to 4cm (1½in) wide, fragrant at night, borne mainly in summer, but intermittently throughout the year if warm enough. Forked, leathery pods containing fleshy-coated red seeds may follow the flowers.

TULBAGHIA
Alliaceae

Tulbaghia fragrans

Origin: *Tropical and southern Africa. A genus of about 25 species of perennials growing from tubers, rhizomes or corms, allied to* Agapanthus *but smelling of garlic when bruised. They have strap-shaped leaves growing from the base of the plant and naked flowering stems topped by umbels of six-tepalled flowers with tubular bases. The one described makes an ornamental pot plant for the conservatory and can be brought into the home when in bloom – if the garlic odour is not objected to! Propagate by division or seed in spring.* Tulbaghia *commemorates Rijk Tulbagh (1699–1771), a popular Dutch governor of the Cape of Good Hope.*

Species cultivated
T. fragrans Sweet garlic South Africa, Transvaal
A clump-forming plant; leaves growing to 30cm (1ft) in length.

Flowering stems are 45cm (1½ft) or more tall carrying umbels of 20 to 40 flowers; each bloom is 1.2cm (½in) long, lilac to mauve, fragrant, mainly summer flowering, but also at other times, even in winter in temperate warmth.

TURRAEA

Meliaceae

Origin: *Tropical to southern Africa, Malagasy, tropical Asia, Australia. A genus of about 90 species of trees and shrubs, a few of which make effective pot plants and specimen flowering shrubs for the conservatory or large room. They have alternate undivided leaves and five-petalled starry flowers growing from their axils. Propagate by seed in spring or by cuttings in summer.* Turraea *commemorates Giorgio della Turre (1607–1688), a Professor of Botany at Padua and author of several books.*

Species cultivated

T. floribunda South Africa

A shrub growing to 2m (6½ft). Leaves are oval, prominently veined, glossy rich green, reaching a length of 8–13cm (3–5in). Flowers are fragrant, palest yellow-green, with very narrow petals 3–4cm (1¼–1½in) long, borne in twos and threes from the leaf axils in spring to early summer.

Turraea floribunda

Vanda tricolor

VANDA
Orchidaceae

Origin: *Tropical Asia. A genus of 60 species of orchids that grow perched on trees (epiphytic) without pseudobulbs. They have erect, often rather woody-based stems, usually unbranched, carrying very narrow leaves in two parallel ranks which can be cylindrical (terete) or flattened. The showy flowers have five similar tepals and a three-lobed, spurred lip, and are borne in erect to arching racemes. They make intriguing house and conservatory plants as long as they can be given good light. The terete-leaved species thrive in full sun and extra humidity. All grow well in pots or hanging baskets. Propagate by removing the top of a leggy plant and taking the shoots from the cut-back plant as cuttings when they have produced aerial roots. Vanda is the Indian (Hindi) name for this orchid.*

Species cultivated
V. parishii (*Vandopsis parishii*) Burma, Thailand
Stems are robust, 15–20cm (6–8in) tall. Leaves are 15–25cm (6–10in) long, oblong-elliptic, the tips bilobed. Flowers are fragrant, growing to 6cm (2½in) wide, fleshy, the tepals yellow to yellow-green spotted with reddish-brown, the lip small, magenta, opening in summer and autumn.

V. suavis See *V. tricolor suavis.*

V. tricolor Java, Bali
The branched stems grow to 2m (6½ft). Leaves are 30–45cm (1–1½ft) long, strap-shaped, leathery and channelled, the tip with two lobes. Flowers are 6–8cm (2½–3in) wide, pale yellow with reddish-brown spotting and a white lip with the central lobe magenta, fragrant; seven to 12 carried on an arching stem up to 30cm (1ft) long, opening in summer and winter.

V. t. suavis
Larger and more freely borne flowers which are white with less heavy magenta to purplish spotting.

VANILLA
Orchidaceae

Origin: *Circum-tropical. A genus of 90 to 120 species of climbing orchids, best known as the source of the vanilla flavouring. The species described here climb by aerial roots and have alternate, thick-textured leaves. The relatively large flowers have similar sepals and petals and a tubular lip. Although not highly decorative, they are well worth trying in the conservatory or large room. Propagate by cuttings of stem sections with three to five leaves in summer. Vanilla derives from the Spanish* vainilla, *a small pod; unlike most orchids, the seed capsules resemble bean pods.*

Vanilla pomponia

Species cultivated
V. planifolia Mexico, Southern Florida, West Indies, Central and northern South America
Stems grow to 10m (33ft) or more in the wild, sparingly branched but easily kept to 2–3m (6½–10ft) with careful pruning. Leaves oblong-elliptic to lance-shaped, slender-pointed, 8–20cm (3–8in) long, sub-lustrous, dark green. Flowers are about 5cm (2in) long, greenish-yellow, growing in short axillary racemes, intermittently all the year if warm enough. Pods are cylindrical, obscurely three-angled, 10–25cm (4–10in) in length. *V. p.* 'Variegata' has the leaves striped and boldly edged with white. The pods of this species provide the main source of natural vanilla.
V. pomponia Mexico, Central America to Brazil
Similar to *V. planifolia*, but the stems are more robust and the leaves longer. Flowers reach a length of 8cm (3in) or more, the lip white or orange. Pods are shorter but considerably thicker.

ZYGOPETALUM
Orchidaceae

Origin: *Central and tropical South America. A genus of about 20 species of mainly ground-growing (terrestrial) orchids which not only have beautiful flowers, but are easy to grow. They form clumps of pseudobulbs, narrow leaves and racemes of comparatively large, often colourful blooms. Each flower has five similar radiating tepals and a large fan-shaped lip of a contrasting colour or pattern. Although best in the conservatory, those described are also worth trying indoors. Propagate by division in spring or after flowering.*

Zygopetalum *derives from the Greek* zygos, *a yoke and* petalon, *petal; a swelling at the base of the lip seems to join or yoke the petals together.*

Species cultivated

Z. intermedium Brazil

The pseudobulbs are egg-shaped to conical and bright green with a sheath over the base, up to 9cm (3½in) tall. Leaves grow in clusters or fans of three to five, lance-shaped elliptic to almost strap-shaped, bright green, arching, 30–45cm (1–1½ft) in length. Flowers are about 8cm (3in) wide, waxy-textured, long-lasting, fragrant, with tepals usually yellow-green blotched red-brown and of more or less equal length; the lip is white with a radiating pattern of purple-red branching veins, the edge waved or crimped; borne in autumn and winter. Frequently grown under the name of *Z. mackayi*. *Z.* 'Marshwood' is a richly hued hybrid.

Z. mackayi Brazil

Much like *Z. intermedium* and often confused with it, but having flowers with the two inner tepals (true petals) noticeably shorter than the others and the veins of the lip near to true red.

Zygopetalum perrenoudii 'Marshwood'

GLOSSARY

Alternate One leaf at each node in a staggered formation up the stem.

Anther The male part of a flower usually consisting of two lobes or 'sacs' containing pollen grains. *See* Stamen.

Areole A tiny hump-like organ found in all true members of the cactus family (*Cactaceae*), which bears bristles, spines, hairs or wool. It arises in what is technically a leaf axil, and is considered to be a highly modified shoot.

Aril An extra external coating around a seed, often fleshy and brightly coloured.

Axillary Growing from the point where a leaf or bract joins the stem.

Bipinnate Of leaves, bracts and stipules that are doubly pinnate, i.e. with leaf lobes that are again pinnate.

Bipinnatisect Of leaves, bracts or stipules that are doubly pinnatisect, i.e. with leaf lobes that are again lobed.

Bract A modified leaf usually associated with an inflorescence, in the axils of which flowers arise. Some bracts are scale-like and insignificant, others are large and coloured.

Bullate Puckered or appearing as if blistered; used of leaves where the tissue between the veins is raised up.

Bulbil Tiny bulbs or compact immature plantlets borne above ground, mainly on the stems of lilies and on the leaves of some other plants.

Calyx The whorl of sepals that protects the flower while in the bud stage.

Capsule A dry, often box-like fruit containing many seeds and opening by pores or slits, or explosively.

Channelled Used of a narrow leaf or leaflet with up-turned edges forming a channel or gutter-shape.

Cone A spike-like structure or strobilus which bears seeds (conifers) or spores (club mosses).

Corm An underground storage organ derived from a stem base.

Corolla The petals of a flower that may be separate or fused to form a funnel, trumpet or bell.

Corymb A racemose flower cluster with the stalks of the lower flowers longer than the upper ones creating a flattened or domed head.

Cultivar Short for cultivated variety and referring to a particular variant of a species or hybrid maintained in cultivation by vegetative propagation or carefully controlled seed production. Such a plant may be purposefully bred by man, or arise spontaneously as a mutation.

Cyme A compound inflorescence made up of repeated lateral branching. In the monochasial cyme each branch ends in a flower bud and one lateral branch. In the dichasial cyme each branch ends in a bud and two opposite branches.

Decumbent Having prostrate stems with the tips erect.

Digitate A compound palmate leaf (like an outspread hand) with the leaflets radiating from the top of the stalk.

Dimorphic Having two forms, e.g. some plants have two distinct types of flowers or leaves on the same plant, others have a different habit when young and adult.

Drupe A fleshy fruit, usually with one central seed.

Elliptic Usually of leaves that are broadest in the middle and taper evenly to the base and tip.

Epiphyte A plant that perches upon another, as orchids and bromeliads grow on trees. They are not parasitic, gaining moisture from rain and air, and food from humus-filled bark crevices.

Floret Tiny flowers, usually when aggregated to form larger ones as in a daisy.

Frond An alternative name for the leaf of a fern or palm.

Genus A category or classification of all living things that groups together all species with characters in common. Of the two basic scientific names which most plants have, the first is the generic, the second the species.

Glochid Tiny barbed bristle on the areole of some cacti.

Habit The general or overall appearance of a plant, e.g. erect, bushy, mat-forming, etc.

Inflorescence The part of a plant that bears the flowers consisting of one or more blooms and their leafstalks and pedicels (the stalk of an individual flower). *See also* Corymb, Cyme, Panicle, Raceme, and Umbel.

Internode The length of stem between two nodes.

Keel The two lower petals of a pea flower (members of the *Leguminosae*), which are pressed together around the pistil and stamens.

Lip The colloquial name for the labellum, the lowest of the three petals in the orchid flower. It is modified in a wide variety of ways to aid pollination by insects.

Lobe A section of a leaf, bract, etc., that is partially separated from the main part of the organ like a cape or isthmus. It is used also for the petal-like divisions at the mouth of a tubular flower.

Monocarpic Of plants that flower and seed once then die. Technically, annuals and biennials are monocarpic, but horticulturally the term is used for plants that live more than two years before flowering.

Mucronate Leaves, bracts, sepals or petals that narrow abruptly at the apex, terminating in a firm, often sharp point.

Nectary A small gland, which secretes a sugary liquid (nectar). Nectaries are found mainly in flowers but sometimes elsewhere such as on leaf stalks.

Node That part of a stem where the leaf is joined and a lateral shoot grows out.

Offset Botanically, a special condensed shoot borne at the end of a short stem from the base of a plant. Horticulturally, also, used of any approximately basal shoot that can easily be detached for propagation purposes. Also used of the small, or daughter, bulbs that form beside the main one.

Opposite Of leaves or other organs borne in pairs on opposite sides of a stem.

Panicle An inflorescence of several racemes or cymes.

Pappus In general, the tuft of hairs on a seed or fruit to assist distribution by wind.

Pectinate Like the teeth of a comb; used of pinnate leaves, bracts or sepals with many narrow leaflets or lobes at right angles to the midrib. Also of leaves, bracts or petals with a fringe of coarse hairs.

Pedate A palmatisect leaf (rounded and palmately lobed almost to the base) with at least two basal lobes again lobed.

Perianth The two outer whorls (calyx and corolla or sepals and petals) that first protect and then display the generative parts. In a general way perianth is used when the petals and sepals look alike as in a tulip.

Pinnate Of a leaf composed of two ranks of leaflets on either side of the midrib.

Pinnatifid A leaf divided pinnately to half up the midrib.

Pseudobulb A swollen aerial stem typical of epiphytic orchids.

Procumbent Lying flat on the ground; in the strict sense, of stems that do not root as they grow.

Raceme An inflorescence composed of a central or main stem bearing stalked blooms at intervals.

Receptacle The usually enlarged stem tip, which bears the floral whorls (petals, sepals, etc.); also the greatly flattened stem tip which bears the florets of daisy or scabious bloom.

Rhizome A more or less underground stem that produces roots and aerial stems. In some cases they are slender and fast growing, in others fleshy with storage tissue and then elongating slowly.

Rootstock Botanically an approximately erect rhizome as found in some ferns. Horticulturally used for the ground-level junction of a compact perennial plant from which roots and leaves or stems arise. Also a horticultural term for a plant or its root system upon which another is grafted.

Scape A leafless flowering stem which arises direct from ground level, e.g. a daffodil.

Sepal The outer whorl of the perianth of a flower, usually green but sometimes coloured and then petal-like.

Spadix A thick fleshy flower spike with the small flowers embedded in pits or sitting flush with the surface; typical of arum lilies and other members of the *Araceae*.

Spathe A green or coloured petal-like bract, which surrounds or encloses the spadix, q.v.

Species A group of individual plants which breed together and have the same constant and distinctive characters, though small differences may occur.

Spore Minute reproductive bodies formed of one or a few cells together, which give rise to new individuals, either directly as in fungi, or indirectly as in ferns.

Sporangium An asexually formed spore.

Stamen The male unit of a flower comprising two anther lobes joined together at the top of a filament (stalk).

Staminode A rudimentary stamen, sometimes functioning as a petal or nectary, but usually producing no viable pollen.

Standard The upper or top petal of a pea flower, or the three inner usually upstanding petals of an iris bloom. Also a gardening term for a tree-like plant with an unbranched main stem and a head of branches.

Style The stalk that joins the pistil to the stigma.

Subshrub A small shrub that is woody at the base only, the upper part, particularly flowering stems, dying back each winter. From a gardening point of view the term is also used loosely for any low-growing softish-stemmed shrub.

Subspecies A distinct, true breeding form of a species, often isolated geographically from the species itself and differing more significantly than a variety.

Syncarp An ovary (later a seed pod or fruit) formed by the fusion of several carpels, e.g. lily, poppy, pineapple.

Tepal Used of petals and sepals combined when they look exactly alike, e.g. tulip, crocus, narcissus.

Trifoliate Mainly of leaves divided into three leaflets, but sometimes used for whorls or groups of three leaves.

Tuber Usually underground storage organs derived from stems and roots. Root tubers, e.g. dahlia, do not produce buds, new growth arising from the base of the existing or old stems. Stem tubers, e.g. potato, bear buds (the eyes of a potato) of which some form the next season's stems.

Tubercle A small wart or knob-like projection on a stem, leaf, or fruit, etc.

Umbel An inflorescence of stalked flowers all of which arise and radiate from the tip of the main stem.

Unifoliate Of plants with one leaf only. Also used of compound leaves (usually pinnate or trifoliate) that are reduced to one large leaflet only.

Variegated The white to cream or yellow markings on leaves due to lack of chlorophyll. Sometimes there are also tints of red, pink or purple. There are three primary causes: mutation, virus infection and a deficiency of an essential mineral which upsets the formation of chlorophyll.

Whorl Of leaves, bracts or flowers arranged in a ring of three or more.